# SPENDING IN THE AMERICAN STATES

AMERICAN POLITICS RESEARCH SERIES

# SPENDING
# IN THE AMERICAN STATES

**IRA SHARKANSKY**
UNIVERSITY OF WISCONSIN

RAND M<sup>c</sup>NALLY & COMPANY · Chicago

# AMERICAN POLITICS RESEARCH SERIES

**Aaron Wildavsky, Series Editor**

Copyright © 1968 by Rand McNally & Company
All Rights Reserved
Printed in U.S.A. by Rand McNally & Company
Library of Congress Catalog Card Number 68:16844

To

the memory of my father

E U G E N E   L.   S H A R K A N S K Y

# ACKNOWLEDGMENTS

Numerous scholars aided the genesis and development of this study by their contributions to the literatures that stirred me to action, by their patient responses to the first utterances of my hypotheses, and by their gracious comments on early drafts. To list all those who participated would impose on the publisher's budget for acknowledgments. Indeed, any listing reveals some pretension on the part of an author. While he is likely to feel that the list bestows rewards, some of those identified might wish to be omitted; and although most authors assert that final responsibility is theirs alone, the listing may relieve them of some of the burden.

In the hope of expressing my thanks, and despite the risk of offending some who are inadvertently omitted and some who are included, I shall list those who read all or part of various manuscript drafts: Geoffrey Y. Cornog, Thomas R. Dye, James Dyson, Frank K. Gibson, Brett W. Hawkins, Richard I. Hofferbert, Herbert Jacob, Clara Penniman, James Robinson, Robert Salisbury, Aaron Wildavsky, Deil Wright, and Bob Zimring. Many of these people have also made invaluable contributions to the literatures on state politics and government expenditures, and thus have performed a double service.

I have acquired several other debts along the way to this book. One is to several professional journals for the opportunity to publish preliminary findings and interpretations: the *Midwest Journal of Political Science,* the *National Tax Journal, Western Political Quarterly,* and the *American Political Science Review.* Another is to government officials and resident political scientists in several states who have given interpretations and further introductions to aid me in my effort to understand deviant cases of state expenditures. The Committee on Governmental and Legal Processes of the Social Science Research Council and the University of Georgia Office of General Research both provided funds necessary for this research.

On the home front, Stefan and Erica supplied many pleasant hours of diversion and, together with my wife, Ina, accepted Daddy's preoccupation with his book.

Athens, Georgia                                                       Ira Sharkansky
September, 1967

# CONTENTS

# LIST OF TABLES

# CHAPTER I

# The Question,
# Possible Answers,
# and Rules of Analysis

THE CENTRAL QUESTION of this book is: Why do some of the American state governments spend more money than others? Although this question appears uncomplicated, the nature of spending processes in the American states makes it necessary to discuss at length the types of expenditures at issue, the types of potential influences on state spending that will be considered, and the analytical techniques that are suited to the investigation.

The subject of state government expenditures is vast in scope and is significant for several interests that are widespread among political scientists. During 1965, the fifty state governments spent a total of $45.5 billion. This sum amounted to $236 per capita and 6.8 per cent of the Gross National Product. In total spending the states rank below both the federal and local levels of government; but when the analysis is limited to spending for domestic functions that all three levels perform in common (thus eliminating the defense and international activities supported by the federal budget), the states rank second in government spending. The figures for 1962, combining both direct expenditures and expenditures given as grants to other governments, are: (1) local governments, 50.2 per cent of the domestic spending of all American governments; (2) state governments, 39.4 per cent; and (3) the federal government, 33.8 per cent.

Obviously, a study of state government expenditures will deal with the allocation of substantial economic resources by public officials. Within each state, officials face questions pertaining to the allocation of resources to state institutions or, by means of intergovernmental payments, to local authorities. At the same time, they also deal with questions concerning allocations between service areas. In the nation as a whole during 1965, state expenditures were distributed among the major services in the following proportions: (1) education, 36.0 per cent; (2) highways, 24.4 per cent; (3) public welfare, 13.5 per cent; (4) health and hospitals, 7.3 per cent; (5) natural resources, 3.1 per cent; and (6) public safety, 2.5 per cent. Yet the officials of each state have made different allocation decisions about the budgets of major agencies. Although the central topic of this book concerns the total expenditures of state governments, it will put this inquiry into perspective by analyzing the total expenditures of each state government in relation to the spending of local governments within its jurisdiction and by analyzing the distribution of each state's funds to the major categories of public service.

A principal interest of political scientists that may be served by an inquiry into state spending is the analysis of relationships among the components of the governmental process and the larger state political system. Spending decisions comprise a vital part of the process, as evidenced by the intense disputes about the magnitude of a state's budget and the distribution of its funds among administrative agencies. Funding is central to government activities. Therefore, an understanding of the factors that influence the level and distribution of spending should illuminate many other happenings at the state level.

Finally, an inquiry into state expenditures may have relevance to political systems outside of the American states. In certain qualities, governmental processes in the states reflect occurrences in other levels of American government or in the governments of other countries. Admittedly, each government is peculiar in many ways; but the findings of a state study can at least supply useful hypotheses for scholars who would investigate comparable phenomena in foreign settings.

At the heart of this book is the idea that expenditure levels respond to certain economic, political, and governmental phenomena within each state. Presumably, decisions to spend money are manifestations of a state's political system at work. These decisions seem likely to respond to the nature of demands and resources that come from the social and economic systems of each state, as well as to internal stimuli from other components of the state political system.[1] The demands received into the

---

[1]The discussion of systems theory relies heavily upon David Easton, *A Systems Analysis of Political Life* (New York: John Wiley & Sons, 1965); Gabriel A. Almond and G. Bingham Powell, Jr., *Comparative Politics: A Developmental Approach* (Boston: Little, Brown & Co., 1966); and Karl W. Deutsch, *The Nerves of Government* (New York: Free Press of Glencoe, 1963).

political system include desires for public services, such as education, highways, welfare, or public safety. The resources of state political systems include the willingness of citizens to comply with tax statutes, the willingness of investors to buy government bonds, the magnitude of federal aids, and the economic wealth available to state revenue measures.

Within a political system, the nature of inputs presumably influences the nature of decisions through *conversion* processes. Factors that affect the conversion of demands and resources into outputs include the *attitudes, perceptions,* and *beliefs* of *participants* in the system, plus the *formal* and *informal rules* that govern their behavior. Mechanisms of *feedback* help to regulate the exchange of stimuli between a political system and its environment. Feedback occurs as the system's activities influence the environment in a way that affects the inputs going from the environment to the political system. The level of spending can affect the nature of services provided, for example, and then influence the demands for additional services which come from interest groups. Thus, decisions of a political system *feed back* into the sensing mechanisms of the system, as the outputs of the system influence its inputs. Through feedback and evaluation, decision-makers may adapt new decisions to the assessed effects that earlier outputs had upon their environment.

As the producer of authoritative decisions, the political system is in a position to make certain contributions to its social and economic environment. Where a society is less "developed" in certain respects than its people desire, the political system may organize the societal resources and provide leadership for change. Social scientists do not agree upon the nature of social-economic-political development, but they do assign a critical role to the political system in several conceptions of development.[2] Political systems may promote changes in the goals that motivate economic or social processes.[3] By raising capital through taxation and channeling it to specific types of investment, the authoritative decisions of government officials may affect the direction and speed of industrial or agricultural change.[4] By using public money to improve the quality and availability of education, the political system can enhance the capacity of individuals to produce economically and enjoy the benefits of increasing wealth.[5] Through the decisions of the political system, society may

[2]See Lucian W. Pye, *Aspects of Political Development* (Boston: Little, Brown & Co., 1966), especially chapt. II.
[3]Deutsch, *Nerves of Government,* p. 253; and W. W. Rostow, *The Process of Economic Growth* (New York: Oxford University Press, 1960), especially chapt. I.
[4]See Paul A. Baran, *Political Economy of Growth* (New York: Monthly Review Press, 1957).
[5]See Mary Jean Bowman and C. Arnold Anderson, "Concerning the Role of Education in Development," in *Old Societies and New States: The Quest for Modernity in Asia and Africa,* edited by Clifford Geertz (New York: Free Press of Glencoe, 1963).

*3*

likewise obtain the public services of transportation, conservation, health and sanitation, public safety, and public administration which contribute to orderly change. At the same time, the government can use its regulatory powers to enforce adherence to established values and thereby stabilize the culture during the period of transition.[6]

Within the political system, public expenditures allegedly reflect the activities of government and provide the wherewithal for the enforcement of authoritative decisions. Whether a particular system happens to be fostering development or conserving an established set of conditions, government expenditures supposedly buy what the government does. Influential writers express the belief that the magnitude of government spending reflects the quality or quantity of public services provided within a jurisdiction. In *1400 Governments,* Robert Wood relies on revenue and expenditure data to "reflect the scope and character of (local) government operations."[7] In his study of highway policy, Philip Burch writes: "Highway policy in the United States revolves around the collection and expenditure of funds. Since money provides the wherewithal for road construction and maintenance, highway finance has been correctly described as 'the beginning and the end, the alpha and the omega.' "[8] And Jesse Burkhead writes: ". . . for the most part, expenditure variations reflect genuine differences in the calibre of educational services provided."[9]

In the face of a widely assumed relationship between spending and service, however, the literature contains a variety of findings that suggest the existence of discrete political entities rather than an extensive system of complementary parts. As Charles Lindblom, Aaron Wildavsky, Thomas Anton, and John P. Crecine describe budgeting, its participants generally seem oblivious of the system-relevant phenomena of popular demands or development of public services. The values of *getting the (budgeting) job done, filling out the forms, keeping next year's appropriation close to this year's appropriation,* or *maintaining the image of severe review* guide the budget decisions of many public officials in the United States.[10] Moreover, the following discussion of the actors in

[6]Robert T. Holt and John E. Turner, *The Political Basis of Economic Development: An Exploration in Comparative Political Analysis* (Princeton, N.J.: D. Van Nostrand Co., 1966), p. 61.

[7]Robert C. Wood, *1400 Governments* (Garden City, N.Y.: Anchor Books, 1961), p. 35.

[8]Philip H. Burch, Jr., *Highway Revenue and Expenditure Policy in the United States* (New Brunswick, N.J.: Rutgers University Press, 1962), p. 34.

[9]Jesse Burkhead, *Public School Finance* (Syracuse, N.Y.: Syracuse University Press, 1964), p. 50.

[10]See Charles E. Lindblom, "Decision-Making in Taxation and Expenditure," in National Bureau of Economic Research, *Public Finances: Needs, Sources and Utilization* (Princeton, N.J.: Princeton University Press, 1961); Aaron Wildavsky, *The*

budgeting decisions suggests that state government officials, in particular, may lack the resources or the inclinations necessary to operate the budget as a political vehicle to provide leadership for the society.

## ACTORS IN STATE EXPENDITURE DECISIONS

The argument that is implicit in much of the following analysis asserts that economic and governmental characteristics of the American states leave only limited discretion to individual budget-makers. But before designating the measures of state government expenditures and the factors likely to influence state-by-state differences in spending, it may be helpful to describe the actors who are directly involved in the expenditure decisions of most states. By learning the titles of principal actors and something about their formal powers, the reader may acquire a rough institutional map that will help him through the abstractions in later pages.[11]

The most prominent participants in spending decisions are executives in the operating agencies, personnel in the central budget office, the governor, and members of legislative committees that review appropriations. In most states, the governor and his chief budget officer have official responsibility for preparing a budget for submission to the legislature from the requests made by operating agencies. The chief budget officer's title may be Finance Director, Budget Director, Comptroller, Commissioner of Administration, or some variation of these. In six states, however, the governor participates in budget-making through a multimember board. In Florida and West Virginia, the governor is chairman of a budgeting group that includes the separately elected Secretary of State, Comptroller, Treasurer, Attorney General, Superintendent of Public Instruction, and Commissioner of Agriculture. In Mississippi, North Dakota, and South Carolina, the governor is chairman of a group that contains separately elected administrative heads plus the chairmen of legislative finance committees and members of the legislature who are named by the presiding officers. The governor of Indiana has only indirect access to budget-making; his appointee sits on a board with legislators who are appointed by the presiding officers of the House and Senate. In 13 other states, the governor works with a chief budget officer

*Politics of the Budgetary Process* (Boston: Little, Brown & Co., 1964); Thomas J. Anton, *The Politics of State Expenditure in Illinois* (Urbana: University of Illinois Press, 1966); and John P. Crecine, "A Computer Simulation Model of Municipal Resource Allocation" (paper delivered at the meeting of the Midwest Conference of Political Science, April 1966).

[11]The following discussion relies upon information supplied in Council of State Governments, *The Book of the States, 1964–65*, pp. 156–67.

who is either separately elected or chosen by the legislature or civil service commission.

Committees in each house of the legislature (or a joint committee), appointed by the presiding officers, typically review the budget that is presented to the legislature by the governor or other executive review body. Most legislatures have wide discretion in changing the budget. However, constitutional provisions earmark certain revenues for certain agencies (e.g., motor fuel taxes to the highway department), or require that revenue match expenditures. In Maryland and West Virginia the legislatures may reduce the funds for any unit but increase only those recommended for the legislatures themselves or, as in West Virginia, for the judiciary. In Nebraska a simple majority may reduce the governor's recommendations, but a three-fifths vote is necessary to increase them. Once the legislatures pass appropriations bills, 49 governors may accept or reject entire bills and 40 governors may reject individual items of appropriations bills. The governor of North Carolina has no veto power.

The findings of numerous empirical studies about the participants in government expenditure decisions agree in assigning primary roles to administrators in the operating agencies.[12] Administrators have the best knowledge of existing programs, and they are most familiar with the discrepancies between current programs and the programs that additional funds might support. Administrators formulate original budget requests and defend their requests before reviewers in the executive and legislative branches. The reviewers have the power to alter requests, but they typically rely upon the administrators' testimony. Agencies usually request more than their current appropriation and receive cuts from the reviewers. But the reviewers seldom cut below the level of previous expenditures.

The literature suggests that administrative primacy in expenditures is more likely to occur at the state than at the federal level in the United States. In the federal government, executive and legislative reviewers have significantly greater resources than their counterparts at the state level.

[12]See the works of Aaron Wildavsky and of Thomas Anton cited in note 10; see also Rufus P. Browning, "Innovative and Non-Innovative Decision Processes in Government Budgeting" (paper delivered at the annual meeting of the American Political Science Association, September 1963); Arthur Macmahon, "Congressional Oversight of Administration," *Political Science Quarterly,* 58 (June and September 1943): 161–90, 380–414; Elias Huzar, *The Purse and the Sword* (Ithaca, N.Y.: Cornell University Press, 1950); Warner R. Schilling, Paul V. Hammond, and Glenn H. Snyder, *Strategy, Politics and Defense Budgets* (New York: Columbia University Press, 1962); Ira Sharkansky, "Four Agencies and an Appropriations Subcommittee: A Comparative Study of Budget Strategies," *Midwest Journal of Political Science,* 9 (August 1965): 254–81; and Ira Sharkansky, "An Appropriations Subcommittee and Its Client Agencies: A Comparative Study of Supervision and Control," *American Political Science Review,* 59 (September 1965): 622–28.

Members of the Congressional Appropriations Committees retain their seats for many years and acquire a level of expertise in the affairs of agencies likely to be far greater than that enjoyed by members of state appropriations committees. Individual state legislators generally have fewer years of legislative experience than members of the federal Congress, and the state legislators are even less likely to have experience with budgeting.[13] While members of Congress hold their seats on the Appropriations Committees by virtue of their seniority, members of state legislative committees generally have no seniority rights in this matter. With fresh members of the appropriations committees appointed at the start of each term, the state legislature is often much inferior in expertise to the administrators who seek funds. Also, at the federal level the executive review of agency requests proceeds under a leadership that is relatively single-minded. The President shares his budgeting responsibilities with no other executive who is separately elected or appointed. The President names his Director of the Bureau of the Budget without a requirement for Senatorial review. Moreover, the Federal Bureau of the Budget can reinforce the President's budget with a number of auxiliary devices that are unavailable to most state budget offices. The Budget Bureau has formal authority to block agency requests to Congress and to regulate the flow of money from the Treasury to agencies after Congress has made appropriations.[14] In dealing with agency expenditures, few state governors or legislative committees possess such supervisory resources as exist at the federal level. It seems unlikely, therefore, that state governors or legislatures can exert pervasive influence over expenditure decisions within their states.

## RELEVANT LITERATURES OF EXPENDITURES ANALYSIS

Where the subject of analysis includes concepts as broad and diffuse as "state government expenditures" and "systems" of economic, social, and political phenomena, there is much room for dispute about the specific topic of study. The critical questions are: *What measurements will be used to analyze state government expenditures? What social, economic, and political phenomena should be tested for their relationships to the measures of state spending?* To enable the reader to appreciate the analytic choices that will prevail throughout the substantive chapters of this book, it will be helpful to review three bodies of literature. Much of

[13]See Thomas R. Dye, "State Legislative Politics," in *Politics in the American States,* edited by Herbert Jacob and Kenneth N. Vines (Boston: Little, Brown & Co., 1965).

[14]See Richard E. Neustadt, "Presidency and Legislation: The Growth of Central Clearance," *American Political Science Review,* 48 (September 1954): 641–71.

this literature does not consider government expenditures at the state level *per se,* but it does have direct relevance for a systems approach to state spending. Each group of writings reflects different selections of dependent and independent variables. Once the reader is aware of the existing field of knowledge, he can better understand the variables that this book considers.

The first approach to the question of state government spending is found in the publications of scholars who have attempted to explain interstate variations in the combined spending of state and local governments within each state. The second body of literature includes the findings of political scientists who have examined interstate variations in the magnitude of government expenditures and other "outputs of state political systems." A third group of publications demonstrates a decision-making approach to the factors that influence individual budget-makers.

## A. The Spending of State and Local Governments

The work that has set the style for many analyses of government expenditures is Solomon Fabricant's *The Trend of Government Activity in the United States Since 1900.*[15] Fabricant uses multiple correlation and regression analysis to define the relationship between three socio-economic measures (per capita income, population density, and the percentage of the population living in urban places) and interstate variations in the per capita expenditures of state and local governments. He finds that high (or low) scores on the independent variables occur with high (or low) scores on per capita expenditures. Using data for 1942, Fabricant finds that variations in the socio-economic measures account statistically for 72 per cent of the interstate variation in total expenditures and for 29 to 85 per cent of the variation in expenditure for major functions. Of the three independent variables, per capita income shows the strongest relationship to expenditures.

Glenn W. Fisher repeats Fabricant's analysis on 1960 state and local government per capita expenditures and compares it with the results of another analysis that employs two measures of economic resources (percentage of families with less than $2,000 annual income and yield of a representative tax system for each state as a percentage of the United States average); three demographic variables (population per square mile, percentage of the population in urban places, percentage increase in population); and two socio-political variables (an index of two-party competition and the percentage of the adult population with less than five

[15]Solomon Fabricant, *The Trend of Government Activity in the United States Since 1900* (New York: National Bureau of Economic Research, 1952).

years' schooling). Fisher finds that his variables explain more of the interstate variation in state and local government per capita expenditures than Fabricant's variables. But, like Fabricant, Fisher finds that his measure of citizens' income shows the strongest individual relationship to state and local expenditures. Neither Fabricant nor Fisher tries to explain in detail the linkage between citizens' income and the expenditures of state and local governments. In an article in the *National Tax Journal,* Fisher ventures to say only that "one possibility . . . is that low-income persons feel tax pressures more keenly and thus resist increases in governmental expenditures more strongly than persons with larger incomes. The generally regressive nature of state and local tax systems would, of course, reinforce any such tendency if it exists."[16]

Seymour Sachs and Robert Harris add to the Fabricant literature by considering the effect on state and local government expenditures of two additional variables: per capita federal aid to state governments and per capita state aid to local governments.[17] With these variables, Sachs and Harris increase the explanation of government expenditures. While Fabricant's three variables explain about 50 per cent of the interstate variation in expenditures in 1960, and Fisher's seven variables, added to the three Fabricant variables, explain about 65 per cent, the two Sachs-Harris variables, added to the three Fabricant variables, explain about 87 per cent of the variance in state and local government per capita expenditures in 1960. Sachs and Harris explain the influence of *federal aid* on state and local expenditures as being the attraction of "outside money" to government officials. By providing only a portion to total expenditures from their own funds, state and local authorities can fund extensive projects that come within the scope of federal grant-in-aid programs. *State aid* represents the use of statewide sales, income, or excise taxes to fund programs that otherwise would rely on the less popular local property tax. Also, state aid may act to increase expenditures by reducing the competition among adjoining local governments to keep taxes low in order to increase their industrial appeal. Even in the Sachs-Harris study, however, the measure of citizens' income remains the most powerful of the independent variables. Moreover, Sachs and Harris provide no more complete explanation than Fisher or Fabricant for the imposing influence of citizens' income over the expenditure decisions of state and local government officials.

[16]Glenn W. Fisher, "Interstate Variation in State and Local Government Expenditures," *National Tax Journal,* 17 (March 1964): 57–73.

[17]Seymour Sachs and Robert Harris, "The Determinants of State and Local Government Expenditures and Intergovernmental Flow of Funds," *National Tax Journal,* 17 (March 1964): 75–85.

Characteristically, the Fabricant group of scholars focuses inquiry upon the numerical results of statistical analysis. Their publications fail to explain how the most powerful correlates of state and local government expenditures actually work upon the public officials who make spending decisions.[18] Part of their problem is an insistence upon combining the expenditures of state and local governments. They do this, presumably, in order to "correct" for interstate variations in the responsibilities of state and local governments.[19] It is true that states vary in these responsibilities. However, when they combine the spending of state and local governments, the researchers fuse the decisions of many separate authorities. As a result, they mask real political processes and lose the opportunity to gain an understanding of financial decisions at either state or local level. When scholars combine state and local government expenditures and find that expenditures show stronger relationships with economic than political variables (e.g., measures of intergovernmental aid or party competition), they may be finding only that the artificial aggregate of state and local government expenditures does not respond to measures of discrete state or local political processes.

The focus throughout this book is on the expenditures of state governments alone. The results uncover two principal phenomena that remain hidden to writers who combine the expenditures of many governments: (1) economic measures show *negative* relationships with several measures of state government expenditures, and (2) state government expenditures show weaker relationships with economic measures than with measures pertaining to governmental phenomena. These findings, in contrast to high positive relationships between economic resources and state and local expenditures, seem to reflect the more flexible revenue positions of state as opposed to local governments. State constitutions generally restrict local governments to the tax on real property. But the local property tax is hard-pressed to produce sufficient revenues under depressed conditions. Most states enjoy the use of productive taxes on personal income and retail sales. And state revenue systems cover a more extensive economy than any local government and can tap the resources of wealthy communities to make up for the lack of resources in poor communities. In poor states, therefore, while local spending and the combined spending of local and state agencies are low, the spending of the state alone may be relatively high. Also, the poor states tend to be southern states with a long tradition of relatively centralized govern-

[18]Elliott R. Morss, "Some Thoughts on the Determinants of State and Local Government Expenditures," *National Tax Journal,* 19 (March 1966): 95–103.
[19]See James A. Maxwell, *Financing State and Local Governments* (Washington: Brookings Institution, 1965), p. 2.

ment. For many years, state governments in the South have assumed a larger than average share of the bills for the public services that are offered by state and local governments. History, as well as economics, seems to influence a high reliance on *state* expenditures in the economically underdeveloped regions of the country.

## B. Outputs of Political Systems

Several political scientists have compared the influence of economic and political phenomena upon the outputs of state political systems.[20] The outputs examined have included measures of government expenditures and government revenue, distribution of revenue between state and local governments, incidence of federal aid, and measures of public service quantity and quality. The political influences tested include a limited collection of indicators for party competition at the state level, the strength of Democratic and Republican parties, the turnout of citizens eligible to vote, and the equity of apportionment in the state legislature with respect to urban and rural districts. Against the influence of these factors on outputs, political scientists have compared the influence from the economic factors of citizens' income, education, urbanization, and industrialization. Correlation techniques have generally shown positive relationships among measures of party competition, voter turnout, and outputs. High (or low) scores on competition and voter turnout tend to correspond with high (or low) scores on the measures of expenditures, revenues, and public service. In the presence of economic measures as control variables, however, party competition and voter turnout lose much of their significant relationship with measures of output. Thus, economic phenomena appear to exercise more basic influences over expenditures, revenue, and services than do party competition or voter turnout. The measures of equity in legislative apportionment show little association with the measures of output.

Several problems reduce one's confidence in the claim that political phenomena have less influence than economic characteristics on government outputs. One problem lies in the lack of specificity with respect to independent and dependent variables. Some variables, such as measures of revenue, federal aid, or government structure, that pose as measures

[20]See Thomas R. Dye, *Politics, Economics, and the Public: Policy Outcomes in the American States* (Chicago: Rand McNally & Co., 1966); Richard E. Dawson and James A Robinson, "Interparty Competition, Economic Variables, and Welfare Politics in the American States," *Journal of Politics,* 25 (May 1963): 265–89; Richard I. Hofferbert, "The Relation between Public Policy and Some Structural and Environmental Variables in the American States," *American Political Science Review,* 60 (March 1966): 73–82.

of system output seem better suited to use as independent political variables that might influence the outputs of public services. A related problem is the limited range of politics included among the independent variables. Omitted from the collection of likely political influences are measures of interest-group activity, federal aid, and tax revenue, and the structure of the civil service. Finally, an insensitivity to the division of responsibilities between state and local governments may affect the results. Most of the output indicators reflect the combined activities of state and local governments, but some pertain to state activities alone, and some are not labeled clearly. At the same time, the political measures pertain only to state affairs. The measures of politics, therefore, assess a different arena of behavior than most measures of output. Local officials, who help determine the combination of state and local outputs, may not be sensitive to the degree of party competition or the strength of individual parties at the *state* level, to the equity of apportionment in the *state* legislature, or to the turnout of voters for *state* elections. Chapter IV of this book tests the relationships between party strength, party competition, legislative apportionment, voter turnout, and state government expenditures. The results are different in detail from those already reported in the literature for combined outputs of state and local governments, although Chapter IV does agree in finding little influence for party strength, party competition, apportionment equity, or voter turnout on state government expenditures. Yet measures of other attributes that may be termed political (measures of previous expenditures, tax revenue, and the division of financial responsibilities between state and local governments) outweigh economic factors as correlates of state government spending.

## C. Financial Decision-Making

Several writers have attempted to describe the decisional criteria of government budget-makers. Three of their findings have particular significance for the analyses in subsequent chapters:

(1) A small group of government officials who have budgetary responsibilities in the administration and the legislature make the basic financial decisions.

(2) The criteria employed by financial decision-makers *do not* reflect a primary concern with the nature of the economy, the platforms of political parties, or articulated policy desires that might be called "urban," "rural," "conservative," "business," "labor," or the like. The criteria of financial decision-makers are non-ideological and frequently non-programmatic.

(3) The primary consideration of financial decision-makers is the level of previous expenditures for each agency and the increases in revenues forecast for the coming period.

Insofar as the "base" of previous expenditures is a political concept, this third group of writers stands distinctly apart from those who argue that economics provide the basic stimuli of government expenditures. As it is employed in spending decisions, the "base" of previous expenditures represents the sum of past decisions, habits, earlier accommodations among important public officials, or widely accepted practices in the arena of financial decisions. In the case of every state budget system examined by this author, for example, the paperwork done by officials in the agencies, central budget offices, and legislatures enforces a concern with previous and current spending and the increment over those levels that is proposed for the coming year. The base serves as the starting point for new calculations by those who ask for funds, and as the portion of a request that is most likely to be considered legitimate by those who review appropriations.

Charles Lindblom makes a major contribution to the understanding of public finance by his analysis of *rational-comprehensive* decision-making. In a number of publications[21] Lindblom has catalogued the shortcomings in the often-prescribed style of decision-making that requires an actor to recognize the whole range of alternatives that is possible, identify his goals, rank his preferences for each alternative, define the resources necessary for each alternative, and make his selection on the basis of all relevant information. Lindblom sees this approach to decision-making (including budgeting) as failing to take into account the limitations of intelligence, time, and policy discretion that actually are available to public officials. Constraints of time and intelligence restrict an official's capacity to identify the full range of alternatives and resources that are available at the point of decision. And the constraints of organization and politics limit the explication of long-range goals and the clear preference ranking of alternatives; the announcement of intentions may arouse conflict among participants who might otherwise agree on specific proposals.

Because rational-comprehensive decision-making is impractical, even though desirable in the view of many public officials, a number of writers have identified alternative styles. An approach that unites the views of several authors is *incrementalism*. As it is discussed here, incrementalism borrows from Lindblom's discussion of "partisan mutual

---

[21]See Lindblom, *Decision-Making;* "The Science of Muddling Through," *Public Administration Review,* 19 (Spring 1959): 79–88; and *The Intelligence of Democracy* (New York: Free Press of Glencoe, 1966).

adjustment" and from Aaron Wildavsky's "partial view of the public interest."[22] The term incrementalism is employed in order to emphasize the relationship of this decision style to budgeting and the fixation of budgeteers on the *increment* between the appropriation of the previous year and the appropriation that is being requested.

Decision-makers who follow an incremental approach to their selections fail to consider all alternatives that face them; they do not announce their goals; they do not rank-preference all the alternatives that face them; and they do not make their decisions on the basis of *all* relevant information. Rather than consider all aspects of an agency's budget during the annual review, incrementalists generally accept the legitimacy of established programs and agree to continue the previous level of expenditure. They limit their task by considering only the increments of change proposed for the new budget and by considering the narrow range of goals embodied in the departures from established activities. The expectations discussed in incremental decision sessions tend to be short-range, pragmatic, and non-ideological. The immediate results for specific groups rather than the long-run significance for society are the most salient concerns.

The principal advantages that Lindblom sees in incrementalism are its compatibility with the limitations of human actors and the opportunity it provides for flexibility in the presence of conflicting demands. As Lindblom explains it, incrementalism is particularly suited to a pluralistic society where the debate is not about grand theories of history that Americans strive to reify once and for all time, but about the claims of participants who seek minor changes in established activities. While increments rather than major changes are at issue, diverse interests can participate in the process without posing major threats to each other. Incremental changes do not commit a program against subsequent modifications and the satisfaction of once-disappointed contenders.

Aaron Wildavsky adds specificity to the concept of incremental budgeting. In *The Politics of the Budgetary Process,* Wildavsky describes the strategies pursued by federal budgeteers as they play the roles typical of their offices: the agency personnel as advocates of program expansion; the Budget Bureau as Presidential servant with a cutting bias; the House Appropriations Committee as guardian of the Treasury with a cutting bias; and the Senate Appropriations Committee as a responsible court that hears appeals from the decisions of the House Committee. Like Lindblom, Wildavsky feels it impractical for an actor to consider seriously all the alternatives before him when he considers a budget request.

[22]See Wildavsky, *Politics of the Budgetary Process,* chapt. 5, especially pp. 165–67.

Officials limit their considerations to those values that pertain to the "roles" they choose to play. Wildavsky defends the cutting biases of the Budget Bureau and the House Appropriations Committee as "making sense in the context of agency advocacy."[23] In light of the cutting biases pursued earlier in the annual budget process by the Budget Bureau and the House Appropriations Committee, it also makes sense for the Senate Appropriations Committee to sympathize with the claims of the agency. Finally, since agency officials feel they know most about the needs of their programs and expect reductions from the Budget Bureau and the House of Representatives, it makes sense for them to be expansive in their requests. To deal with conflicts in a manner consistent with democratic pluralism, Wildavsky feels that each actor's "partial view of public interest" is more desirable than a "total view of the public interest." When a participant speaks for his own bias, Wildavsky feels there is *less* danger of omitting important values from the final decision than when participants neglect the values in their immediate view in favor of what they think is a total view; and because the participants generally remain close to the base of previous activities, their posture toward program expansion or budget cutting does not preclude the temporarily dissatisfied from having their desires reconsidered at a later time.

Thomas J. Anton describes the decision rules used by principal participants in the Illinois budget process.[24] As Wildavsky found at the federal level, Anton finds primary attention given to an agency's base of existing appropriations and the increment of new requests; and more than Wildavsky, Anton finds decision-makers relying on a set of simplistic rules that reveal little concern for program-related values. Decisions depend almost entirely upon the dollar value of agency requests as they compare with previous budgets and upon the reviewers' estimates of the tax revenue to be available in the coming biennium. Inasmuch as reviewers tend to cut new requests without regard to their effect on programs, agency officials in Illinois expand services by shifting expenditures from one program to another within budgets that remain stable in their total funds.

Several factors help explain the lack of concern for programs among budget reviewers in Illinois. Both the governor and the legislative committees have little staff assistance to investigate the program implications of a budget; and the values of reviewers sacrifice program development to "economizing." If single-minded economizing reflects decision rules that are found widely in state governments, it is unlikely that state expenditures will reflect the nature of party activities, legislative apportionment,

[23]*Ibid.*, p. 163.
[24]See Anton, *Politics of State Expenditure*, pp. 253–55.

voter turnout, or economic conditions. Where the value of economizing prevails, the level of current expenditures may relate to nothing more exotic than the level of previous expenditures.

The findings of Lindblom, Wildavsky, and Anton do not indicate that expenditures of particular states will remain fixed in relation to the spending of other states. There is a strong likelihood that current expenditures will vary only marginally from previous expenditures, but there is room in an incremental system for an occasional major change. Lindblom, Wildavsky, and Anton do not analyze the stimulants of major changes in a systematic fashion, but they do suggest some stimulants. Technological advances might produce "breakthroughs" in particular services that make investments in new staff or facilities desirable; or changes in the public's attitudes toward a service may stimulate sharp increases; and new federal grants may provide a justification for major departures by state budget-makers. It appears that recent increases in state expenditures for mental health have responded to a related combination of new technology (e.g., promising developments in drug therapy), awakened public support for mental-health activities, and new federal grants. Even in the presence of these formidable stimulants, however, it may be necessary for a principal actor in the budget process (e.g., the Chief Executive) to take an extraordinary interest in an agency's program in order to obtain a major budget increase. State budget mechanisms include a number of actors who play major parts in the agencies, the central budget office, the governor's office, and the legislature; and a negative inclination on the part of any of them can present a severe barrier to an increase in spending.

There is little to suggest that the stimulants of change in incremental budgeting are generally present phenomena subject to easy measurement and analysis. A variety of particular conditions, such as the interests of individual participants, the availability of new federal programs, technological change, or a combination of political happenings that generate a "ripe" legislative opportunity, may precede major changes. There are enough separate participants in each state's budgetary process to make it unlikely that one particular factor (e.g., "economic development") will have a similar effect upon the expenditures of many states at any one time. While economic changes may affect certain officials in each state, anything less than a major depression or inflation may fail to elicit similar responses from the variety of officials who must respond.[25]

[25]A study of correlates of changes in combined state and local government expenditures found that economic measures are less able to account for interstate variations in expenditure change than for interstate variations in current expenditures. See Roy W. Bahl, Jr., and Robert J. Saunders, "Determinants of Changes in State and Local Government Expenditures," *National Tax Journal,* 18 (March 1965): 50–57.

Thus, there is an apparent conflict between the first two bodies of literature and the third, with the first two suggesting a clear impact of economics on government expenditures and the third citing no continuing influence beyond the politically legitimated base of existing spending, which is, on occasion, subject to change from political or economic stimuli. Yet the findings of this book show certain similarities to each of the literatures discussed. The factor that shows the closest relationship to each state's level of current expenditures is its expenditures in the recent past. Nevertheless, other measures pertaining to economic and governmental characteristics of each state also show significant relationships with the measures of current state spending and measures of change in spending. As noted above, however, these relationships differ considerably from the findings obtained when the subject of analysis is the combined expenditures of state and local governments.

## THE SUBJECTS OF EMPIRICAL ANALYSIS

The precise definitions of state government expenditures that are used in this book vary from one analysis to another. In most contexts, however, the examination deals with *general government expenditures* as the dependent variable. General government expenditures is a concept developed by the United States Bureau of the Census. It *excludes* expenditures for state liquor stores and insurance trust funds and permits the comparison of different states' spending for the services that are provided most generally by state governments. The services that bulk largest in general expenditures are education, highways, public welfare, health and hospitals, natural resources, public safety, and general government. The category of natural resources includes agriculture, conservation, forestry, fish and game, and parks. Public safety includes the functions of police, corrections, and parole. General government includes the support of the state legislature and judiciary, financial administration (tax collection and budgeting), and the administration of employment security programs.[26] In most analyses, absolute expenditures are divided by the population of each state in order to produce *expenditures per capita*. If this correction were not made, it would be found that the sheer size of population bore a very close relationship to the sheer magnitude of government spending.[27] The per capita convention, in frequent use among social scientists, permits the examination of relative expenditure levels among the states.

[26]U.S. Bureau of the Census, *Compendium of State Government Expenditures, 1965* (Washington: U.S. Government Printing Office, 1966), pp. 51ff.
[27]Wood, *1400 Governments*, p. 35.

Later chapters consider six classes of potential influences on the magnitude of government expenditures in the American states.

(1) Governmental characteristics;

(2) Political characteristics that reflect ways in which citizens may gain access to government decisions;

(3) Economic and social characteristics of state populations that seem likely to influence their "needs" for state expenditures or their capacity to provide the revenues needed for state expenditures;

(4) National and international happenings that seem likely to affect the economic resources available to state officials;

(5) The regional affiliation of state governments that may represent the norms of services, taxes, and expenditures that have prevailed historically for state decision-makers;

(6) Public service levels in the states that present demands on budget-makers for financial support.

Both "governmental" and "political" categories of potential influences on state expenditures fit into the "political system" concept that is widely accepted among political scientists. They are given separate designations here, however, in order to separate a class of variables, i.e., governmental characteristics, that has not received adequate consideration in the existing literature.

The governmental characteristics that seem likely to weigh heavily on state budget-makers include the level of previous expenditures, the revenues available from taxes and federal aids, financial relationships between state and local governments, and the nature of the state bureaucracy. The inclusion of previous expenditures reflects the importance given this item in the descriptions of financial decision-making. In the writings of Lindblom, Wildavsky, Anton, and Crecine,[28] previous expenditures represent the base where budget-makers start in calculating their new requests. The base stands as the sum of past accommodations, habits, or activities that go unchallenged in the periodic budget review. When administrators submit their requests for a new fiscal year, they typically use forms that require them to list previous appropriations and to justify any increase that is requested. For executive and legislative review bodies, the base is the portion of a request most likely to be considered legitimate; their inquiry typically focuses on the part of a budget that differs from previous appropriations. The statistical relationships between previous expenditures and current expenditures are very strong. Yet the influence of the past is not total. While the influence of previous

[28]See works cited in note 10 above.

expenditures has served to temper the magnitude of increase at each budget review, factors other than previous expenditures have worked in favor of increases in spending. State expenditures have increased many times over during the twentieth century. However, because of the profound relationship between current and previous levels of spending, these relationships themselves are the subject of Chapter III. The other governmental variables, plus the state economic and political variables, are considered together in Chapter IV.

The items of state revenue that are examined for their relationships to current spending include the proportion of state revenue received from the federal government, the percentage of citizens' personal income paid in state taxes, and the prominence of various taxes (e.g., general sales, excise, and personal income) in the state revenue system. Presumably, the magnitude of each revenue source will show positive relationships with the level of state government spending.

Measures of financial relationships between state and local governments show the proportions of state and local funds that are raised or spent by state government agencies and the level of local government spending within each state. These measures reflect the financial assistance that citizens and local government officials receive from state or local agencies, and thereby set the parameters of state government activity. Studies that combine the expenditures of state and local governments overlook interstate differences in the divisions of financial responsibilities. This book looks upon the rules governing these divisions as a factor of potentially crucial importance in the definition of state government spending. It is expected that state spending is high where the rules assign a heavy share of the state-local financial responsibilities to state agencies.

Measures relating to the state government bureaucracy show the relative number of state employees and their average salaries. The size of the bureaucracy should reflect the magnitude of the state government establishment and the size of an interest group (state employees) that typically demands improved salary and working conditions from budgeteers. Employees' salaries and other personnel costs consumed an average of 19.4 per cent of state expenditures during 1962; thus, the number and salaries of state employees may represent important positive correlates of total spending.

The *state economic system* seems likely to influence expenditures by its effect on the needs and resources of state populations. While peaks and valleys may occur in the national economy, some states are always wealthier than others. Several economists and political scientists have shown that levels of per capita personal income, population, industrialization, and urbanization correlate with the *combined expenditures of state and local governments.*[29] It is not necessary for the economic situation to show similar relationships with the expenditures of state governments alone. During the depression, state governments showed themselves to be less vulnerable than local governments to economic conditions. The restrictions of state constitutions confine local governments to certain types and levels of taxes; as a result local units rely almost exclusively on the unpopular property tax. In contrast, state officials have a relatively wide choice of tax levels and tax bases. Moreover, state governments have access to wealthy economic segments of their population; broad-based taxes can redistribute resources from "have" to "have-not" areas. States also enjoy direct access to an extensive set of federal grants. By carefully choosing among their alternative sources of revenues, state officials may bypass constraints coming from their own economies. Chapter IV assesses the relationships among state expenditures and components of the state economic system. It shows important negative relationships between economic conditions and state spending and explains this finding by reference to the division of responsibilities between state and local governments that prevail in poor and wealthy states.

The literature of political science contains a number of expectations about the influence on government expenditures from certain components of state political systems that pertain to citizen-government relationships. With higher-than-average levels of voter turnout, interparty competition, and equitably apportioned legislatures, citizens should have a greater-than-average opportunity to make their desires known to government officials.[30] Because citizens generally favor improved public services, it is expected that high scores on these traits are associated with high levels of state expenditure. Indeed, several writers have found positive simple relationships among the incidence of voter turnout, the intensity of interparty competition, and the combined expenditures of state and local governments. However, these simple relationships have disappeared when controlled for the presence of economic characteristics.[31] Thus, the existing finding is that economic resources have a more direct bearing on state and local government spending than the political traits of voter turnout and party competition. In order to test this finding for state governmental expenditures, Chapter IV compares the statistical relationships between state spending and measures of political, governmental, and economic characteristics.

[29]See works cited in notes 15 to 20 above.
[30]See Dawson and Robinson, "Interparty Competition"; Dye, *"Politics"*; and Hofferbert, "Relation."
[31]*Ibid.*

20

National and international events that have an economic impact seem likely to affect the spending of state governments. During the depression of the 1930's, the national economic system cut severely into the property base of state taxation, and 23 states adopted retail sales taxes.[32] The depression also triggered huge increases in federal grants for public welfare and natural resources. Finally, the depression crippled many local governments and increased the legal responsibilities of state agencies. Economic trauma associated with World War II and the Korean War added to the cost of state services through inflation and cut down the supplies of manpower and material. In postwar years, postponed demands for war-neglected services and population increases added to demands upon state governments. Some demands and responses are still occurring two decades after the war's end. Recent increases in state expenditures for education reflect, in part, the arrival of war babies at the age for college and graduate school.[33] Chapter V documents the impact of depression and war on state government expenditures and finds that the depression, in particular, shook the fabric of state expenditure processes with sufficient force to upset established patterns of spending.

There are several reasons to expect regional cultures to influence state expenditures. Several studies of state party systems and electoral processes claim to discern regional peculiarities in culture, economics, and/or political history which influence political actors.[34] Such factors may also influence state spending. Moreover, officials affiliate with their counterparts from neighboring states in a number of professional organizations. Through contacts made in national and regional meetings, state officials come to regard officials in nearby states as sources of information that are helpful in planning their own activities. As a result, the consultive patterns of government officials may reinforce the tendencies of neighboring states to adjust their services, taxes, and spending to regional norms. In an attempt to assess the impact of regional affiliation on

[32]John F. Due, *State Sales Tax Administration* (Chicago: Public Administration Service, 1963), p. 3.

[33]See R. A. Musgrave and J. M. Culbertson, "The Growth of Public Expenditures in the United States, 1890–1948," *National Tax Journal,* 6 (June 1953): 97–115; Frederick C. Mosher and Orville F. Poland, *The Costs of American Governments: Facts, Trends, Myths* (New York: Dodd, Mead & Co., 1964); and Myron Slade Kendrick, *A Century and a Half of Federal Expenditures* (New York: National Bureau of Economic Research, 1955).

[34]See, for example, V. O. Key, *Southern Politics in State and Nation* (New York: Alfred A. Knopf, 1949); Duane Lockard, *New England State Politics* (Princeton, N.J.: Princeton University Press, 1955); John H. Fenton, *Politics in the Border States* (New Orleans: Hauser Press, 1957); and John H. Fenton, *Midwest Politics* (New York: Holt, Rinehart & Winston, 1966).

spending, Chapter VI compares average state expenditures in 14 regions of the United States and compares the relationships between spending and certain governmental characteristics from one region to another.

The nature of public service outputs may also affect government expenditures. Not uncommon is the belief that the magnitude of government spending reflects the quality or quantity of public services. As noted above, several authors have identified expenditure levels with service levels. None of these authors actually tests the relationship between services and expenditures. Indeed, some of their own data fail to show the relationships that they posit.[35] Certain technical problems preclude the test of relationships between measures of public services and the expenditures of state governments. However, Chapter VII considers the more general service-expenditure relationship by assessing public services within each state and combined expenditures of state and local authorities.

As political wholes with distinct cultures and political personalities, the states are lost in most of the pages that follow. The focus is upon expenditures and a small number of abstractions that appear likely to explain interstate differences in spending; characteristics of the states are removed from their contexts and arrayed on tables for statistical investigation. Although the principal findings suggest limits to the influence that individual people, dramatic historical experience, and state oddities exert on the spending decisions of state governments, this does not mean that peculiarities of state culture or political personalities have no relevance for expenditures. Chapter VIII considers individual cases where personalities or recent historical experiences seem to outweigh the principal independent variables in their influence on state spending. Its findings suggest that, while such instances are rare, they show the opportunities open for individuals to upset established spending patterns.

## THE NATURE OF DATA AND STATISTICAL TESTS

This book relies almost entirely on information collected by government and private organizations for a variety of governmental, commercial, and scholarly purposes. Most of the data comes from publications of the United States Census Bureau and other agencies of the federal

[35]Burkhead, for example, includes data that fail to show the assumed relationships between four measures of expenditures for education and likely indicators of program "caliber," such as the salary of beginning teachers, the insurable value of school capital per pupil, and the number of full-time employees in auxiliary services (counselors and medical personnel). See Burkhead, *Public School Finance*, pp. 50–75.

government.[36] These agencies collect a wealth of information pertaining to state government expenditures and the economic, social, and political phenomena likely to be associated with state spending. The advantages of this information include its ready availability, the use of categories that facilitate state-by-state comparisons, and considerable prior use by other social scientists. These features render the data inexpensive, well suited to the comparative orientation of this book, and tested in previous research. There are certain disadvantages that result from the scarcity of trustworthy non-quantitative data and from the heterogeneity of purposes that guided the original data collections. No systems analyst with an Eastonian orientation appears to have made authoritative decisions about data gathering. Available publications do not provide measurements for each of the components that appear theoretically relevant to the expenditure process. Some of the data assess the theoretical categories only indirectly. In the case of spending figures, the diversity of state government organization has discouraged the Census Bureau from collecting information about each agency's budget; the Bureau reports spending in the artificial (but comparable across state lines) categories of education, highways, public welfare, health and hospitals, natural resources, public safety, and general government. Finally, the agencies that publish the information do not collect it directly; they rely upon the willingness and capacity of agencies in each state to interpret and complete the mailed questionnaires accurately.

Although the nature of information used in this book cautions a skeptical posture toward the analysis, it should not discourage the pursuit of inquiry. The study proceeds on the assumption that further analysis using non-quantitative techniques or additional quantitative information might complement or alter the findings reported below. Intellectual humility is essential in the absence of good numbers for everything, but the humility should not stifle work that is possible at the present time. One's confidence in the data used here should increase as it becomes apparent in following chapters that relevant aspects of the expenditure process are measured satisfactorily and that findings are sensible in relation to what is widely known about politics in the American states.

Each analysis in this book employs analytic tools that have enjoyed wide previous use with the type of problems to be investigated. No student should hesitate to proceed if he has a minimum of knowledge of independent and dependent variables, means, standard deviations, coefficients of simple and partial correlation, and coefficients of multiple determination. A *variable* is a characteristic that literally varies from

[36]The sources for the data employed in this book are shown alongside each indicator and variable in the Appendix (see pp. 155–66).

23

one occasion of measurement to another. The variables used in this study are measurements of state government expenditures and the characteristics that seem likely to be associated with expenditures as potential influences upon them: federal aid, tax effort, previous expenditures, and so on. These characteristics vary from state to state at any one point in time and within states from one point in time to another. A *dependent variable* is a subject of analysis that is likely to vary in response to independent variables. That is, a dependent variable is one whose value (score) depends on the values of independent variables. The principal dependent variables of this study are measures of state government expenditures. The *independent variables* are those characteristics identified by theory as likely to influence state government expenditures. *Means* (averages) define general tendencies among groups of states on individual variables, and *standard deviations* (a measure of the dispersion of scores about their means) show the degree of consistency within each group. *Coefficients of simple correlation* (Pearson's r) show the strength and direction of relationship between two variables (e.g., federal aid and state expenditures). If the direction of the relationship is positive, it means that high (or low) scores on one variable are associated with high (or low) scores on other variables. Thus, states scoring high on federal aid would also score high on expenditures. Where correlation coefficients are negative, they signal inverse relationships between variables: high scores on one variable coexist with low scores on the other variable. The magnitude of correlation coefficients ranges between $+1.0$ and $-1.0$. The closer the coefficient to plus or minus 1.0, the greater the relationships between scores on the variables. In graphic terms, a simple correlation coefficient of $+1.0$ reflects the condition where each state's scores on two variables plotted on two axes at 90 degrees from one another form a straight line at 45 degrees from the horizontal. Inversely, a coefficient of $-1.0$ reflects a plotted line 135 degrees from the horizontal. A correlation coefficient approaching 0.0 reflects a plot that shows no linear pattern of relationship between two variables.[37]

Coefficients of simple correlation do not indicate if relationships between variables are truly *independent*. That is, they cannot determine if a relationship between federal aid and expenditures indicates an elemental relationship between aid and spending or merely reflects a more basic relationship involving a third variable, e.g., a measure of economic resources. If an economic measure has powerful relationships with both federal aid and current expenditures, then the relationship between fed-

[37]The variables employed in this study pass the tests required by correlation analysis: they are each interval in nature; their distributions approximate normality; and all two-variable relationships are linear.

eral aid and current expenditures may reflect nothing more than the existence of the common factor. *Coefficients of partial correlation* help to indicate the independence of relationships. When used in a multivariable problem, they show the strength of relationships between two variables while taking into account their common relationships with others. Coefficients of neither simple nor partial correlation indicate the success of several independent variables in explaining interstate differences in a dependent variable (e.g., current expenditures). *Coefficients of multiple determination* show the percentage of interstate variation in a dependent variable which is explained by a combination of independent variables. Where other statistical techniques are employed for special purposes, they will be explained as they are introduced.

By themselves, the statistical techniques used in this book do not indicate relationship of *causation* or *influence*. A relationship between *A* and *B* does not mean that *A* influences *B*. The hypothesized designation of "independent" and "dependent" variables may be inaccurate. *B* could influence *A*; or *A* and *B* could both respond to the mutual influence of untested factors. Yet the argument will leap beyond the confines of statistics and speak of influences exerted by some factors upon others. When this occurs, the statistical evidence only indicates that the influence *could exist*. The author's confidence in his political and economic sense—as explained to the reader—provides the fundamental basis for going beyond statistical inference.

## CHAPTER II

# Comparative Research in the American States

THE FOCUS of this book—the identification of factors that determine why some state governments spend more than others—requires the comparison of expenditure levels with other political, governmental, economic, and social characteristics of the American states. But before the techniques of comparative analysis can be exercised in a legitimate fashion, it is necessary to determine if the governments of the states are sufficiently distinct from one another to permit separate sets of conditions to influence their spending. Second, it is necessary to examine their economic, social, and political characteristics to determine if the ranges of state scores are sufficiently broad to permit the reasonable conclusion that differences in environmental characteristics effect differences in state spending.

As its first task, this chapter examines the linkages between federal, state, and local authorities to determine if the *state governments* are sufficiently distinct as governmental entities to be the subjects of comparative analysis. By asking if the states are distinct, this question seeks to determine whether there are meaningful boundaries around the expenditure processes of individual state governments.

The easy access of state agencies to federal grants-in-aid and the opportunities for state officials to influence the nature of federal grant programs through their contacts in Congress represent mechanisms for redistributing wealth among the states that go beyond any. arrangements for international assistance. Inasmuch as federal aid has an effect on each state's expenditure decisions, the expenditure system of Alabama is not entirely distinct from the expenditure system of California.[1] Moreover,

[1]Thomas R. Dye, *Politics, Economics, and the Public: Policy Outcomes in the American States* (Chicago: Rand McNally & Co., 1966), pp. 292–93.

each state government receives demands from local governments in its jurisdiction. Thus, the states are not governmental islands. They respond to stimuli from their common federal government and from the myriad of local governments within their own jurisdictions.

Despite the interlocking of governmental organizations that characterizes the American federal system,[2] it is useful and legitimate to analyze the abstraction labelled "state government expenditures." One of the benefits of systems theory is that it permits analyses that are not bound to organizational frameworks. As conceived in this book, the state expenditures of Alabama are distinct from those of California. The processes that determine each state's expenditures receive inputs of federal money and the programmatic demands that accompany the money, and each receives demands and resources coming from local governments; but inputs from federal and local sources are not the same for each state. Furthermore, because of peculiarities in each state's political and economic characteristics, influences from federal agencies and local authorities do not affect each state in the same manner.

The American federal system is sufficiently flexible for state governments to maintain considerable individuality in the face of increasing federal activities. Among the factors that protect state autonomy, the formal guarantees included within the United States Constitution may be the least potent.[3] The extra-constitutional bulwarks of state autonomy include: (1) state-based political parties; (2) "civil societies" coterminous with states' borders that use the institutions of state government to pursue societal goals; and (3) the increasing ability of state governments to satisfy their citizens' needs for public services.

The American party system has roots within the states and serves to protect state interests in national councils.[4] Unlike their counterparts in Great Britain, elected officials in the United States do not owe principal obligations to national party leaders who may block their renomination or reelection. Members of the United States House of Representatives and Senate owe their major debts to party organizations and individuals within their states. Similarly, aspirants for a Presidential nomination must win the support of party officials in a number of critical states.

Populations in American states have demonstrated loyalty to their own civil societies in the face of outside pressures. The response of south-

[2]Morton Grodzins, "American Political Parties and the American System," *Western Political Quarterly,* 13 (December 1960): 974–98.

[3]Much of the following discussion relies on Daniel J. Elazar, *American Federalism: A View from the States* (New York: Thomas Y. Crowell Co., 1966), chapt. 1.

[4]See Grodzins, "American Political Parties," and Theodore H. White, *The Making of the President 1960* (New York: Atheneum Publishers, 1961), pp. 135–49.

ern states to federal civil rights enactments demonstrates concerted activities on the part of state officials, local governments, and private organizations. In another sphere of cooperation, diverse groups in every state—Chambers of Commerce, elected officials, economic development agencies, Representatives in Congress, and individual businessmen—work to obtain federal contracts for industries or federal expenditures on military installations and public works for their state.

The viability of state party systems and civil societies helps to maintain and improve the ability of state governments to provide public services. While the federal government may render a wider range of services directly to individuals than ever before, the states also are doing more than in the past. Some of the states' money comes from federal agencies along with obligations to meet certain federal standards. But even the federally aided programs provide administrative discretion to the recipient agencies. No studies have found that state governments are losing powers generally by receiving federal grants. Federal programs often support "new" activities that permit state agencies to provide services not previously supported with state funds; and the states share certain decisions with federal administrators in these new programs. If "power" is defined as the ability to control one's environment, then increased knowledge, technological ability, and economic resources permit federal *and* state governments to increase their powers.[5]

Not only are state governments improving their service offerings by means of federal grants, but the states themselves continue to innovate. North Carolina devised training programs for the poor which helped in the development of federal anti-poverty programs; Wisconsin's experience with income tax administration, beginning in 1911, helped in the development of new revenue systems in other states and at the federal level; during the 1930's, Mississippi led in the development of sales taxation as a revenue producer that is relatively insensitive to economic crisis; and officials of several state governments have engaged in the travail of removing the death penalty from their criminal codes. Even the field of civil rights, often the subject of federal intervention, has received substantial state attention. Over 30 state legislatures preceded the federal Congress in passing legislation to protect the political and economic opportunities of minority group members. Now other state govern-

[5]If one accepts this definition of power, then it also appears that individuals are improving their power position in society, in comparison to previous generations, as they acquire more education, more real income, and the resulting greater opportunities to control their own lives. Thus, power itself is an increasing phenomenon. An increase in the power of the federal government does not require a decrease in the powers of other governments or individuals.

ments, including some members of the old Confederacy, have taken significant voluntary steps to protect minority rights.[6]

While the states seem to show enough distinctiveness as governmental units to provide fit subjects of comparative analysis, it is necessary to establish that they differ among themselves on characteristics thought likely to influence differences in expenditures. If the states show a prevailing similarity in any governmental, political, economic, or social characteristics, their scores on these characteristics could not be said to affect their level of expenditures.

Although cross-national differences in definitions of the measurements make a precise comparison on more than a few variables impossible, it is evident from a reading of Tables II–1 and II–2 that variations within the United States are great enough to overlap worldwide variations on most characteristics of personal income, urbanization, population growth, health care, and voter turnout. Relative to the world mean, the United States is more urbanized, more stable in its population increase, and more fortunate in the wealth of its people, the rate of literacy, access to physicians, and participation in national elections. In none of these characteristics, however, is the United States a world leader. And in several characteristics it does not vary from the world mean by so much as one standard deviation. (See Table II–1.)

Within the United States, there is considerable variation in governmental characteristics that are important for the understanding of state government expenditures. On the item of total expenditures per capita, Wyoming spent more than two and one-half times the level of New Jersey in 1962. State taxes in New Mexico have taken twice the percentage of personal income as they have in New Jersey; the incidence of state government employees is more than twice as great in Delaware and Vermont as it is in New Jersey; and the state government of Vermont spends over twice the percentage of state-local revenues as does the state government of New Jersey. (See Table II–2.) Although the low scores of New Jersey may appear unique in this brief recitation, that is not the case. New Jersey is merely an extreme case among several state governments that show consistently low scores on expenditures per capita, the incidence of government employees, tax effort, and the state share of state-local financial responsibilities.

There are also qualitative differences among the states in governmental characteristics that might affect expenditures. Almost all of the states share the traits of constitutionally distinct executive, legislative,

[6]Elazar, *American Federalism,* pp. 207–8.

TABLE II–1

The United States in the International Context

| | United States | World High | World Low | World Mean | Standard Deviation |
|---|---|---|---|---|---|
| Gross National Product per capita | $2,577 | Kuwait ($2,900) | Nepal ($45) | $377 | 474 |
| People per physician | 780 | Israel (400) | Ethiopia (117,000) | 1,508 | 2,522 |
| Percentage of population in cities of over 20,000 people | 52.0% | Hong Kong (81.9%) | Liberia (0) | 23.1% | 18.2 |
| Annual population increase | 15.2% | Costa Rica (38.1%) | Luxembourg (4.0%) | 19.7% | 10.4 |
| Voters in recent national elections as percentage of voting-age population | 64.4% | U.S.S.R. (99.6%) | Several nations (0%) | 57.1% | 30.0 |

SOURCE: Bruce M. Russett *et al.*, *World Handbook of Political and Social Indicators* (New Haven: Yale University Press, 1964).

TABLE II–2

Differences among the American States

| | High State* | U.S. Average | Low State* |
|---|---|---|---|
| Personal income per capita, 1962 | Nevada ($3,278) | $2,366 | Mississippi ($1,285) |
| Infant mortalities per 1,000 live births, 1962 | | | |
| White | Wyoming (29.7) | 22.3 | Delaware (17.9) |
| Non-white | South Dakota (54.2) | 41.4 | Idaho (23.5) |
| People per physician | New York (518) | 749 | Alabama (1318) |
| Percentage living in "urban" communities of at least 2,500, 1960 | New Jersey (88.6%) | 69.9% | North Dakota (35.2%) |
| Percentage living in standard "metropolitan statistical areas" with central cities of at least 50,000, 1960 | Rhode Island (86.3%) | 63.2% | Vermont Idaho (0.0%) Wyoming |
| Annual population increase, 1950–60 | Florida (78.7%) | 18.5% | West Virginia (−7.2%) |
| Percentage housing facilities dilapidated or lacking one or more plumbing facilities | Mississippi (48.9%) | 18.2% | California (6.8%) |
| Percentage Selective Service registrants passing mental examination, 1962 | Utah (95.3%) | 79.7% | South Carolina (45.4%) |
| Voters as a percentage of voting-age population in elections for U.S. Representative, 1962 | Idaho (66.5%) | 46.9% | Mississippi (13.7%) |

TABLE II–2 (Continued)

|  | High State* | U.S. Average | Low State* |
|---|---|---|---|
| State government expenditures per capita, 1962 | Wyoming ($283.69) | $181 | New Jersey ($110.47) |
| State taxes as a percentage of personal income, 1965 | New Mexico (9.2%) | 5.4% | New Jersey (2.7%) |
| Percentage of state-local revenue allocated to state government | Vermont (59.7%) | 33.8% | New Jersey (25.0%) |
| State employees per 10,000 population, 1962 | Delaware Vermont (139) | 80 | New Jersey (56) |

*Excluding Alaska and Hawaii.

and judicial branches of government, of a bicameral legislature, of the use of counties as administrative districts, and of an executive budget. However, the content of these institutions varies widely among the states. The salary and other perquisites of legislators differ enough to have a likely impact on the nature of people who contest for seats.[7] Governors vary in the staff resources and prerogatives pertaining to the budget, in discretion in appointing subordinates, in the number of terms they are allowed to remain in office, and in the extent of their veto powers.[8] And administrative agencies differ from state to state in the salaries and welfare benefits offered to prospective recruits and in the use of partisan or professional criteria for selecting personnel.

In their economic, social, and political characteristics the American states are arrayed along ranges that are broad enough to permit the reasonable conclusion that differences in these characteristics may effect differences in state government expenditures. In per capita personal income, Nevada has a score two and one-half times that of Mississippi. On a commonly used measure of education (the percentage of selective service registrants passing the mental examination), Utah's score is more than

[7]John G. Grumm and Calvin Clark, *Compensation for Legislators in the Fifty States* (Kansas City, Mo.: Citizens Conference on State Legislatures, 1966).
[8]Joseph A. Schlesinger, "The Politics of the Executive," in *Politics in the American States,* edited by Herbert Jacob and Kenneth N. Vines (Boston: Little, Brown & Co., 1965), pp. 207–38.

twice that of South Carolina. On measures of health, non-white children in South Dakota show a mortality rate about three times that of white children in Delaware; and New Yorkers have more than twice the relative number of physicians of Alabama. On a measure of housing quality, the percentage of inadequate homes in Mississippi is seven times as great as in California. In a widely used voting index, adults in Idaho vote at a rate almost five times as great as those in Mississippi.[9] The findings of this book may not have universal relevance, but they may at least have meaning for a significant sample of countries where characteristics fall within the ranges encompassed by the characteristics of American states.

Although it is beyond the scope of this book to compare the phenomena of state expenditures with those of other countries, several factors suggest that the result may be worth the effort. First, it may be true that the financial aids offered to states by the national government of the United States are both more generous and more predictable than the foreign receipts obtained by the national governments of the world. However, this does not obviate the expectation that income from foreign sources has an impact on government expenditures the world over. As in the case of the American states, these payments may bulk largest in the expenditures of the least wealthy countries, and there may be a positive relationship between changes in the level of foreign receipts and changes in the level of public expenditures.

Second, no sovereign government is isolated totally from dependence on the demands and resources of local government bodies. All major governments of the world coexist with local authorities that are legally subordinate to the central jurisdiction, but retain certain discretionary powers of their own. As in the case of the American states, it seems reasonable to hypothesize that the proportion of financial responsibilities assumed by central (as opposed to local) authorities will influence the spending levels of the central government.

Third, the expenditures of most national governments seem likely to be dependent, at last partly, upon the economic resources within their jurisdiction, upon the productivity of their revenue systems, and upon the level of previous expenditures. However, national governments—like state governments in the context of this book—seem capable of drawing upon a more extensive and varied economy than are local governments within their jurisdiction. As a result, the spending of central governments

[9]This chapter makes no attempt to show ranges of all the variables used throughout the book. A few have been chosen for illustrative purposes either because they are particularly important in the empirical analysis or because they show close resemblance to indicators for which international data are available. As noted in Chapter I, each of the variables employed in the chapters that follow meet the requirements of the analytic techniques that are used.

the world over may be less dependent than local governments upon the average level of economic resources within their borders.

Although the particular variables suitable to international analysis may differ from those employed in this study, the following hypotheses—reflecting the findings of later chapters—seem worthy of cross-national consideration: (1) positive relationships exist between the proportion of national resources paid in taxes and the expenditures of central governments; (2) the expenditures of central governments are less dependent on the average level of available economic resources than are the expenditures of local governments; and (3) strong positive relationships prevail between current and previous expenditures of national governments. To the extent that international research yields markedly different results on these dimensions than the domestic research that is reported here, it will appear that the American states do operate in a peculiar political-economic context. In the absence of clear evidence, however, one should avoid any claims of uniqueness.

## SUMMARY

This chapter deals with two questions about the utility of comparing the expenditure phenomena of the American states. The first inquires if the state is a political unit with sufficient independence from federal and local governments to make it a worthwhile focus of comparative analysis. The second asks if the governmental, economic, social, and political characteristics of the American states are sufficiently varied to support an inquiry that posits interstate variations in these characteristics as being critical to interstate variations in expenditures.

There is persuasive evidence that state governments have sufficient autonomy to be suitable units for comparative analysis and that state economies, societies, and governments are sufficiently varied to provide a rich collection of independent variables. Moreover, there are sufficient variations among the American states to suggest them as suitable units for cross-national research. While the American states may have certain attributes that are unique, they also share social, economic, and political characteristics with many foreign jurisdictions. These shared traits may be of sufficient importance with respect to the phenomena of government expenditures to make the findings of this book useful as provocations of international research.

# CHAPTER III

# State Government Expenditures 1903–1965: The Continuing Influence of the Past

EACH OF THE AUTHORS who are cited in Chapter I as making a contribution to the understanding of financial decision-making highlighted the importance of previous expenditures in the set of decisions that comprise governmental budgeting.[1] When administrators at the agency level plan their requests, they use forms that require them to compare last year's appropriation with current plans and to justify any increase that they request. In making their requests, agency administrators typically compare their own desires with an optimum percentage increase that is derived from cues given to them by superiors through formal letters of instruction or public comments. The cues estimate the anticipated increases in government revenues or comment about the priorities to be enjoyed by various programs. Among officials in the central budget office, in the governor's office, or in the legislative committees, the size of an agency's previous appropriation represents the funds considered necessary to operate its established programs. Last year's budget has a legitimacy in the eyes of these reviewers that protects it in most cases from a searching review. Moreover, the reviewers' own scheduling problems

[1]Charles E. Lindblom, "Decision-Making in Taxation and Expenditure," in National Bureau of Economic Research, *Public Finances: Needs, Sources and Utilization* (Princeton, N.J.: Princeton University Press, 1961); Aaron Wildavsky, *The Politics of the Budgetary Process* (Boston: Little, Brown & Co., 1964); Thomas J. Anton, *The Politics of State Expenditure in Illinois* (Urbana: University of Illinois Press, 1966); and John P. Crecine, "A Computer Simulation Model of Municipal Resource Allocation" (paper delivered at the meeting of the Midwest Conference of Political Science, April 1966).

*35*

serve to protect agencies from investigations directed at established programs. In order to maximize the limited time alloted to budget review,[2] officials in the central budget office and the legislature typically focus their attention on the requests for new funds. They are most likely to direct their questions at the portion of the request that represents an increase in appropriations, and they are most likely to cut these requests in their attempt to keep expenditures in line with anticipated revenues.

In this chapter, the task is to measure the relationship between previous and current state government expenditures. It is expected that the correlation coefficient between current expenditures and those of the recent past will approach +1.00. This will signify that state governments' expenditures stand in approximately the same relationship to one another from one budget period to the next, even though all states may have increased their expenditures during the interim. It is also expected that high but diminishing positive correlation coefficients will exist between state government expenditures in a current year and their expenditures in previous years extending backward in time. While states maintain their relative positions in expenditures over a considerable period of time, it is likely that, as the time period increases between earlier and later spending periods, the opportunities increase for changes to occur in the relative spending positions of different states.

It is necessary to do more than document the rather obvious expectation that the past influences the present in state government expenditures. By expressing the relationship between past and present spending in quantitative terms, this chapter will present the influence over current state expenditures that is available to factors other than the size of previous appropriations. The findings show considerable variation in the strength of the past-present relationship from one field of state expenditures to another. Budgets for education, public welfare, and general government, for example, appear to be bound more tightly to the levels of their previous appropriations than are budgets for highways, health, and hospitals. Also, the strength of the past-present relationship varies considerably from one state to another. During each of the budget periods considered in this analysis, a number of states have shown marked spurts above the level of growth shown by states generally, while other states have lagged behind the prevailing rate of growth. These findings will help prepare the reader for analyses in later chapters which seek

[2]The Council of State Governments reports that the formal budget process in most states allots a mere eight to nine months from the submission of agency requests to the governor until the beginning of the new fiscal year. See *The Book of the States, 1964–65* (Chicago Council of State Governments, 1964), pp. 164–67.

to explain that portion of current expenditures which is not explained successfully by the level of previous expenditures.

While previous expenditures show very close relationships with the level of current expenditures, the level of previous expenditures does not show a close relationship with measures of change in expenditures. The provocations of change are not inherent in levels of previous spending. Later chapters show that changes in expenditures respond to a large variety of factors, including economic resources and needs, political conditions, tax revenues, and the presence of leaders with intense motivations and the political resources to attain their goals.

Although this chapter points to some of the analytic limitations in the notion of previous expenditures, it emphasizes the prominence of prior expenditures in the determination of current spending. The chapter argues that no statistical analysis of current expenditures should proceed without reckoning with the level of previous expenditures. Thus, previous expenditures stand with population size as obvious constraints on state government expenditures which should be controlled while investigating the impact of additional correlates. When Chapter IV considers the impact of economic, political, and governmental variables on state government expenditures, it controls for the influence of both population and previous expenditures.

## TECHNIQUES

This chapter uses several techniques to deal with the following four principal topics of inquiry:

(1) Relationships between past and current levels of state government spending during the 62 years between 1903 and 1965;

(2) Changes in spending during 11 periods between 1903 and 1965;

(3) Changes in the spread among states' spending levels from 1903 to 1965;

(4) Variations among fields of spending and among states in the past-present relationships shown by government spending.

The major tools for topics 1, 2, and 4 are correlation and regression analyses. With coefficients of simple correlation, the following pages show the degree of correspondence between current and past total spending per capita at 11 points of time during the twentieth century. For a recent period of time, correlation coefficients also document relationships between past and current expenditures per capita for the major fields of education, highways, public welfare, health and hospitals, natural resources, public safety, and general government.[3] Correlation techniques also help to identify patterns in spending changes. The measures of change include both percentage changes and changes in total dollars per capita during various periods.

In order to assess changes in the spread of state government expenditures over time (topic 3), this chapter employs coefficients of variability. This statistic represents the standard deviation of state government expenditures in a year divided by the mean (arithmetic average) of state government expenditures in that year:

$$\frac{s.d.X}{X}.$$

The greater the coefficient of variability, the greater is the relative deviation of state expenditures about their mean, and the greater is the spread between high- and low-spending states with respect to the national average.

Finally, a regression analysis identifies variations by individual states from the relationship between past and present spending. This analysis begins with a formula of the type

$$Y = a + bX,$$

where $Y$ is current total general expenditures per capita, $X$ is total general expenditures per capita in the recent past, and $a$ and $b$ are constants that represent changes that occurred generally between past and present expenditures. By multiplying each state's past expenditures by the constant $b$ and adding this product to the constant $a$, it is possible to estimate the state's current expenditures on the assumption that its past-present spending relationship resembles that found generally among the states. Then by comparing this estimated expenditure for the current year to the actual state spending according to the ratio

$$\frac{\text{actual spending}}{\text{estimated spending}},$$

it is possible to identify those states where current spending is markedly above or below the level estimated on the basis of previous spending. Where the ratio between actual and estimated spending approximates 1.00, then the state shows the level of current spending expected on the basis of its previous expenditures; but where the ratio between actual

[3]As noted in Chapter I, the field of natural resources includes the functions of agriculture, forestry, fish and game, and parks; public safety includes police, corrections, and parole-probation; and general government includes the support of the legislature and judiciary, plus the administration of insurance trust funds and financial administration (budgeting and revenue collection).

and estimated spending is substantially above or below 1.00, then the state stands out as one where special factors may have intervened to upset the "normal" past-present spending relationship. In this chapter, the ratios of actual to estimated spending show the frequency of state-by-state variations in the past-present spending relationship and support a discussion about the peculiar spending changes shown by individual states over time. In Chapter VIII, these same ratios identify states where it has been profitable to make brief case studies for the purpose of identifying unusual economic or political occurrences that have intervened in the typical past-present spending nexus.

## FINDINGS

As expected, there is a close correspondence between the relative positions of states' current total general expenditures and their expenditures during the recent past. When current and past years are only three years apart (representing in most cases the expenditures of two consecutive biennial budgets), the coefficient of simple correlation approaches +1.00 in magnitude. For the 1962–1965 period, the data of Table III–1 show a coefficient of .94. For past and present years separated by five years, the data of Table III–1 (Column A) show coefficients in the range of .62 to .88.[4]

As the time interval between past and present expenditures increases, the magnitude of the relationship decreases. This fact suggests that a greater time span between any two sets of expenditure decisions provides greater opportunity for factors to enter the budgeting process which are remote from the context that surrounded the first budgeting period. Government officials generally examine only the immediate past appropriations in the actual deliberations that produce a current budget. Yet even as the time between a current budget period and a year in the past increases, the expenditures of that past year retain their status of legitimacy; they represent the funding for established programs that form the nucleus around which later activities (and expenditures) grow. Table III–1 (Column B) shows coefficients of simple correlation between total general expenditures per capita in 1965 and total general expenditures

[4]The years chosen for this analysis were keyed to the five-year interval between the 1957 and 1962 *Census of Governments*. Before 1942 and after 1962, however, the years were selected on the basis of data availability. Where alternative data were available, those years chosen were meant to approximate five-year intervals between the points of observation. From 1942 to 1965, the data come from the U.S. Bureau of the Census, *Compendium of State Government Finances* for the individual years; from 1918 to 1939, the data come from the U.S. Bureau of the Census, *Financial Statistics of States* for the individual years; for 1903 and 1913, the data are from those years' Census Bureau publications of *Wealth, Debt, and Taxation*.

TABLE III–1

Coefficients of Simple Correlation between Current and Past State
Government Total Expenditures per Capita

| Column A | | Column B | |
|---|---|---|---|
| Years | Simple Correlation | Years | Simple Correlation |
| 1965–1962† | .94* | 1965–1962† | .94* |
| 1962–1957 | .85* | 1965–1957 | .85* |
| 1957–1952 | .87* | 1965–1952 | .85* |
| 1952–1947 | .69* | 1965–1947 | .63* |
| 1947–1942 | .74* | 1965–1942 | .72* |
| 1942–1939 | .87* | 1965–1939 | .61* |
| 1939–1929 | .43* | 1965–1929 | .61* |
| 1929–1924 | .62* | 1965–1924 | .53* |
| 1924–1918 | .66* | 1965–1918 | .49* |
| 1918–1913 | .88* | 1965–1913 | .52* |
| 1913–1903 | .83* | 1965–1903 | .44* |

*Significant at the .05 level.
†The first year listed indicates the "current expenditures"; the second year listed indicates the "past expenditures." The coefficients of simple correlation express the relationship between the two sets of expenditures.

per capita for 11 previous years back to 1903. Expenditures in each of these years show coefficients of simple correlation with 1965 expenditures that pass a common test for statistical significance.[5] This means that interstate differences in spending during 1965 bear a resemblance to the differences that prevailed 62 years earlier! With several major wars and domestic transformations in the economy, together with vast population changes in some of the western and southern states and a manyfold increase in the magnitude of each state's spending, the basic patterns of state spending have remained stable throughout the century. As later chapters show, the states have reacted to national phenomena with vast changes in their spending. Yet states that were high (or low) spenders in 1903 have generally remained high (or low) spenders until the present. Table III–2 identifies the five highest and five lowest spenders of 1965 and demonstrates that most of them have retained their relative positions above and below the national averages throughout the century.

[5]The test for statistical significance is not, strictly speaking, applicable because the 48 states comprise a universe, rather than a sample chosen to represent a universe. However, the test provides a device for identifying relationships that are "sizable."

TABLE III-2

1903–1965 Per Capita Spending Levels of States Scoring in Five-Highest and Five-Lowest Categories in 1965

| | 1965 | 1962 | 1957 | 1952 | 1947 | 1942 | 1939 | 1929 | 1924 | 1918 | 1913 | 1903 |
|---|---|---|---|---|---|---|---|---|---|---|---|---|
| Wyoming | $408.28 | $283.69 | $207.85 | $140.47 | $62.73 | $48.87 | $37.74 | $36.14 | $16.47 | $8.75 | $4.95 | $3.16 |
| Delaware | 372.98 | 246.53 | 205.19 | 176.64 | 68.49 | 49.88 | 41.27 | 40.69 | 16.18 | 4.40 | 4.92 | 2.02 |
| Nevada | 348.45 | 277.06 | 216.11 | 163.47 | 112.61 | 60.67 | 42.84 | 48.41 | 26.32 | 10.98 | 9.97 | 5.94 |
| New Mexico | 334.65 | 238.62 | 213.95 | 137.33 | 98.26 | 46.65 | 29.59 | 27.48 | 10.45 | 5.13 | 2.60 | 1.46 |
| Utah | 313.46 | 208.60 | 132.43 | 104.99 | 83.93 | 49.81 | 40.54 | 22.86 | 13.92 | 8.41 | 5.26 | 3.20 |
| U.S. average | 230.53 | 181.40 | 136.64 | 98.31 | 63.09 | 36.93 | 27.34 | 20.61 | 9.88 | 5.23 | 3.68 | 2.24 |
| South Carolina | 172.81 | 141.80 | 108.40 | 85.36 | 55.71 | 28.21 | 17.30 | 15.66 | 5.26 | 1.82 | 1.27 | .82 |
| Texas | 163.22 | 137.21 | 103.20 | 74.75 | 39.12 | 24.89 | 20.51 | 16.18 | 7.92 | 4.59 | 2.97 | 2.26 |
| Nebraska | 154.32 | 125.49 | 93.70 | 72.87 | 47.50 | 27.72 | 17.01 | 12.69 | 6.06 | 3.86 | 2.60 | 1.88 |
| Ohio | 149.54 | 130.34 | 106.20 | 73.95 | 49.53 | 37.46 | 30.16 | 9.96 | 4.85 | 3.50 | 2.29 | 1.65 |
| New Jersey | 123.93 | 110.47 | 83.17 | 77.09 | 61.62 | 29.21 | 21.26 | 22.56 | 11.19 | 6.85 | 4.66 | 2.56 |

The sample years between which the spending of the past bore the *least* resemblance to that of the present were 1929–1939. While the coefficient of correlation for this period is strong enough to be considered significant, it is markedly lower than that shown for any of the other periods. Some of this peculiarity may result from the relatively long time span involved. Most other periods reported in Column A of Table III–1 are five years or less. Yet findings reported later suggest that the relatively low coefficient between 1929 and 1939 expenditures reflects a real-world phenomenon of importance. The Great Depression imposed severe strains on the revenue-spending processes in many states. Existing state property taxes suffered markedly along with the value of real property; many states adopted new taxes and several generous federal programs began operation. A number of local governments found their limited revenue systems unable to cope with the depression, and the financial responsibilities of state governments increased accordingly. Findings reported later in this chapter show that the spread between the high and low spending states decreased noticeably during the 1930's. Thus, it appears that great spending changes during the 1929–1939 period are reflected in the relatively low coefficient of simple correlation between 1929 and 1939 spending.

The relationship between past and present spending is not of equal strength in all fields of government activity. Table III–3 shows coefficients of simple correlation between 1957 and 1962 general expenditures per capita for the fields of education, highways, public welfare, health

TABLE III–3

Coefficients of Simple Correlation between
Current and Past Expenditures, by Field of Service, 1957–1962

|  | *Current Expenditures for Field of Service* |
| --- | --- |
| Past expenditures for: |  |
| Education | .93* |
| Highways | .63* |
| Public welfare | .93* |
| Health and hospitals | .84* |
| Natural resources | .78* |
| Public safety | .70* |
| General government | .95* |

*Significant at the .05 level.

and hospitals, natural resources, public safety, and general government. The relationships are greatest in the fields of education, public welfare, and general government, and are weakest in the highway field. These differences reflect the nature of program changes occurring in these fields during the 1957–1962 period. These years saw significant changes in highway financing, with considerable expenditures stimulated by federal money for the Interstate and Defense Highway System. Perhaps because some states took advantage of these federal funds more rapidly than others, the 1962 pattern of spending differed from that of 1957. Spending for general government in 1962 shows the greatest resemblances with spending in 1957. This constancy may reflect the relative stability in the activities included within the field. General government expenditures during 1962 included money to support the legislature and judiciary (22 per cent of the funds), employment security administration (35 per cent), and financial administration (45 per cent). Compared to other areas of state government activity, these fields escaped vast substantive changes that would be powerful enough to upset established spending patterns. Likewise, spending patterns in the field of public welfare remained stable during the 1957–1962 period. This finding may reflect the resistance to innovation among professional social workers and state welfare administrators prior to 1962 which Gilbert Y. Steiner describes in his *Social Insecurity: The Politics of Welfare*.[6] Spending patterns in the education field also appear to have remained relatively stable from 1957 to 1962. While education spending at the state level increased faster than total general expenditures during this period (19 per cent increase in education and 15 per cent increase in total spending), no development appeared capable of upsetting interstate variations in spending for education. Perhaps educational administrators throughout the country are so attuned to new developments that most states adopt service (and spending) innovations at about the same time. The result of such a practice would mirror the present findings: great increases in educational expenditures along with stability of interstate differences in educational spending between 1957 and 1962.

There has been an overall narrowing of the spread between high- and low-spending states during the 1903–1965 period. Table III–4 presents the means, standard deviations, and coefficients of variability for the per capita total general spending for 12 separate years. This table does not correct for differences in inflation over time or for differences in the magnitude of the economic resources from which governments draw

[6]Gilbert Y. Steiner, *Social Insecurity: The Politics of Welfare* (Chicago: Rand McNally & Co., 1966).

their revenues. Thus, it does not support meaningful inferences about the magnitude of changes in average state government expenditures from 1903 to 1965. Chapter V deals with the topics of changes in *real spending* during this century. However, the coefficients of variability for individual years do support inferences about changes in the spread of high- and low-spending states around the national average.

Although the spread between high- and low-spending states is much less now than at the beginning of the century, its lessening has not occurred as a steady, progressive phenomenon. The diversity between high and low spenders decreased from 1903 through 1929, took a relatively large step in the 1929–1939 period, and then continued at a slower pace until 1962. The 1962 and 1965 coefficients of variability show that the differential between high- and low-spending states *increased* during that period. This represents an aberrant case or the beginning of a trend counter to that in operation since 1903.

Several happenings may be responsible for the long-run 1903–1962 lessening of the spread between the high- and low-spending states. During that period, there has been some evening of economic resources among the states, increases in the federal supports designed to help the poorer states, and the development of nation-wide norms of public services, tax levels, and state government expenditures. These norms re-

TABLE III–4

Means, Standard Deviations, and Coefficients of Variability
for Total State Government Expenditures per Capita

|       | Mean     | Standard Deviation | Coefficient of Variability |
|-------|----------|--------------------|----------------------------|
| 1965  | $230.53  | 60.72              | .27                        |
| 1962  | 181.40   | 41.48              | .23                        |
| 1957  | 136.64   | 35.88              | .26                        |
| 1952  | 98.31    | 27.29              | .28                        |
| 1947  | 63.09    | 17.52              | .28                        |
| 1942  | 36.93    | 9.93               | .27                        |
| 1939  | 27.34    | 8.63               | .32                        |
| 1929  | 20.61    | 8.44               | .41                        |
| 1924  | 9.88     | 4.37               | .44                        |
| 1918  | 5.23     | 2.25               | .43                        |
| 1913  | 3.68     | 1.65               | .45                        |
| 1903  | 2.24     | 1.12               | .50                        |

ceive their support from national organizations of state government officials and from federal agencies that provide financial assistance to the states. State officials from operating agencies and central budget offices, plus elected executives and legislators, affiliate with one another in national and regional organizations that serve as communications media among state governments. Federal agencies promote interstate uniformity in services and spending by means of formal requirements for the receipt of federal funds and informal suggestions made to state officials. The rash of federal programs begun during the Great Depression may have made a special contribution to the marked shrinkage of interstate spending differentials that occurred between 1929 and 1939. Another factor at work during the depression was the diminished productivity of local property taxes and compensatory increases in the spending responsibilities of state governments. This occurrence—to be discussed in Chapters IV and V—may have had a telling effect on the spending levels of many state governments that previously had been low spenders.

Although it is too early to determine if the increased dispersion between high- and low-spending states during the 1962–1965 period represents a temporary aberration or a lasting departure from the narrowing of the spread that has occurred throughout the twentieth century, it is possible to isolate the field in which the 1962–1965 spread took place. Table III–5 shows coefficients of variability for spending during 1962 and 1965 in the major fields of education, highways, and public welfare; these fields account for 73.5 per cent of state spending during 1962. The coefficients indicate that it was primarily in the highway field that the dispersion of high- and low-spending states occurred. It is in the highway field that federal aid bulks largest, both in the amount of dollars received by states and in the statistical relationship between federal aid received and state expenditures. Perhaps the federal programs that were available during the 1962–1965 period were particularly attractive to states that already were high spenders in that field; if so, the grants would contribute

TABLE III–5

Coefficients of Variability for State Government Expenditures per Capita, by Major Field

|                | 1965 | 1962 |
|----------------|------|------|
| Education      | .38  | .36  |
| Highways       | .48  | .39  |
| Public welfare | .41  | .42  |

to the recent increase in the spread between high- and low-spending states.

Findings from a correlation analysis of changes in state expenditures complement the evidence above in pointing to 1929–1939 and 1962–1965 as unusual periods of change in the pattern of spending among the states. Table III–6 shows coefficients of simple correlation between changes in total spending per capita during each of eleven periods and the level of total spending per capita in the first year of each period. The measure of change is the dollar amount of difference between the first and last year of each period.[7] There is a strong negative relationship between the 1929–1939 change and the level of state spending in 1929. This indicates that low-spending states made the greatest increases in spending and reflects the marked lessening of spread between high and low states during the depression years, as noted above in the discussion

TABLE III–6

Coefficients of Simple Correlation
between Changes in Total State Government Spending per Capita
and Spending in the First Year of Each Period

| | Spending in First Year of Each Period |
|---|---|
| Change in total spending per capita between: | |
| 1962–1965 | .61* |
| 1957–1962 | —.03 |
| 1952–1957 | .21 |
| 1947–1952 | .07 |
| 1942–1947 | .25 |
| 1939-1942 | .01 |
| 1929-1939 | —.52* |
| 1924–1929 | .12 |
| 1918–1924 | .19 |
| 1913–1918 | .30* |
| 1903–1913 | .26 |

*Significant at the .05 level.

[7]The measure of change is the absolute dollar change in total spending per capita during each period. Measures of percentage change during each period show comparable results, but appear suspect because of the ease with which low-spending states can show the greatest percentage increases.

of Table III–4. The strong positive relationship between 1962 spending and the 1962–1965 change reflects the increase in the spread between high- and low-spending states for those years. The coefficients for the other periods are too small to be statistically significant, with the exception of 1913–1918, where the coefficient just meets the test for significance. Taken in connection with the data of Table III–4, the coefficients of Table III–6 show that the periods of 1929–1939 and 1962–1965 displayed the occasions of greatest change in the relative positions of high- and low-spending states.

One of the factors that seems to hold state governments in their same relative spending positions for many years at a time is their inability to support marked increases in spending (relative to the increases of other states) over a span of several budget periods. States that show considerable increase in one period display relative decrease or stability in a following period. This fluctuation in expenditure changes appears in the data of Table III–7. They are coefficients of simple correlation between percentage changes in expenditures during ten periods since 1913 and percentage changes that occurred during preceding periods. In each instance, expenditure changes show negative relationships with *previous*

TABLE III–7

Coefficients of Simple Correlation between Period Percentage Changes
in Total State Government Expenditures per Capita
and Percentage Changes in Previous Periods

|  | *Percentage Change in Immediate Preceding Period* |
| --- | --- |
| Percentage change between: | |
| 1962–1965 | —.30* |
| 1957–1962 | —.23 |
| 1952–1957 | —.36* |
| 1947–1952 | —.46* |
| 1942–1947 | —.02 |
| 1939–1942 | —.52* |
| 1929–1939 | —.49* |
| 1924–1929 | —.25 |
| 1918–1924 | —.16 |
| 1913–1918† | —.03 |

*Significant at the .05 level.
†Previous period is 1903–1913.

*changes in expenditures.* Along with the information about a continuing increase in state spending (see Table III–4), the data of Table III–7 suggest that the spending of most states has increased in spurts; a period of relative increase following a period of stability or decline with respect to the general upward trend.[8]

The findings of fluctuations in expenditure changes complement the previous findings of close relationship between previous expenditures and current expenditures. Together they suggest that state officials are unable or unwilling to make continued sharp increases in expenditures. Perhaps, after a period of increase, legislators show a limited tolerance for budgets that seek additional growth, or agency heads encounter problems in the continuing process of expanding their operations. Problems associated with expenditure increases include personnel recruitment, organizational adjustments, and changes in agencies' relations with their clients and with legislative and executive overseers. After an increase in expenditures, administrators might try to consolidate gains without seeking budget increases, or legislators might slash whatever proposed increases come before them. After a period of relative stability, in contrast, certain legislators, interest groups, and administrators may build widespread support for budgetary advances.

The findings of alternation between expenditure increase and stability may also reflect the processes of an administration's maturation. A governor or agency head may come into office with new ideas; but after certain program changes (and increases in expenditures), the new administration may exhaust its ideas or political energies. As a result, innovation ceases to be the dominant orientation, and expenditure stabilization or decline follows expenditure increase.

With a lack of continuing spurts (or lags) in expenditure change, most states retain their positions with respect to other states' expenditures. Yet individual states are not bound to previously set spending patterns. Certain states have spurted ahead in spending, while others have lagged behind prevailing rates of growth. By means of regression analysis, it is possible to identify states that have shown unusual changes in expenditures. The analysis employs a regression equation in the form $Y = a + bX$, where $Y$ is the dependent variable (spending), $X$ is the independent variable that is generally most powerful (previous spending), and $a$ and $b$ are constants that account for the change in expenditures that have been general during an era. By using this equation to estimate

[8]It is unlikely that the negative relationships merely grow out of the data employed. Although low percentage change in a state's expenditures during one period may follow high percentage change even though the dollar increments are identical, the continuation of high-low-high-low percentage changes over several periods testifies to the prominence of fluctuations in changes.

each state's expenditures and then comparing estimated expenditures to real expenditures according to the formula

$$\frac{\text{actual expenditures}}{\text{estimated expenditures}},$$

it is possible to identify states that were not in step with the prevailing changes in expenditures between, for example, 1957 and 1962. Where the results of this formula equal 1.00, a state's estimated expenditures equal its actual expenditures. Where the ratio between real and estimated expenditures is more than 1.00, it is apparent that a state's real expenditures are greater than its estimated spending on the basis of its previous expenditures. Where the ratio between real and estimated expenditures is less than 1.00, it is apparent that a state is spending less than was estimated on the basis of previous expenditures. The results of this analysis appear in Table III–8. It shows the ratios of actual to estimated expenditures for total spending in eleven periods between 1903 and 1965. The table arbitrarily labels as *spurts* or *lags* relative to prevailing patterns those instances where actual spending per capita differs from estimated expenditures by at least 15 per cent.

The data of Table III–8 reinforce a number of observations made earlier. It is rare for a state to show continuing rates of marked increase or decrease in expenditures. During the 11 selected periods between 1903 and 1965 (including 528 ratios) there are only 11 consecutive spurts above the prevailing rates of change and 21 consecutive lags behind prevailing change. More common are the instances of alternation between spurt and lag. Table III–8 shows 51 cases where a state followed a spurt by a lag or followed a lag by a spurt. It is most common that actual expenditures resemble estimated expenditures after a spurt or lag. These cases suggest that a state has established a new position following marked changes in spending. Its position, relative to other states, then sets the pattern for later expenditures.

The data for spending by function suggest that instances of marked deviation from patterns set by previous expenditures are unlikely to happen in many of a state's services. Between 1957 and 1962 no state showed marked deviation in more than three of the seven spending fields. The holding power of an expenditure base may be such that it can give way only in a limited number of fields during any one period.

No general explanation seems to fit the large number of deviant expenditures identified in Table III–8. Major innovations in state tax structures preceded several of the spurts. Colorado, Kentucky, Rhode Island, and Utah introduced new broad-based taxes before their spurts above previous spending patterns; and Connecticut increased the rate of

TABLE III–8

Ratios of Actual to Estimated Total State Government Expenditures per Capita

| | 1965 | 1962 | 1957 | 1952 | 1947 | 1942 | 1939 | 1929 | 1924 | 1918 | 1913 |
|---|---|---|---|---|---|---|---|---|---|---|---|
| Alabama | 1.01 | .97 | 1.17* | .92 | 1.06* | .82* | .62* | 1.04 | .81* | .78* | 1.09 |
| Arizona | .98 | 1.03 | 1.00 | .92 | 1.00 | 1.26* | 1.15* | 1.05 | .85* | 1.61* | 1.10 |
| Arkansas | .92 | 1.05 | .96 | .87 | 1.17* | .99 | .42* | 1.39* | 1.08 | .84* | .89 |
| California | 1.00 | 1.00 | 1.01 | 1.19* | .84* | 1.02 | 1.66* | .71* | 1.14 | .95 | .84* |
| Colorado | 1.04 | .95 | 1.01 | .96 | 1.07 | 1.09 | 1.35* | .81* | 1.01 | 1.20* | .75* |
| Connecticut | .92 | .80* | 1.57* | .83* | 1.00 | .99 | 1.00 | .97 | .93 | 1.05 | 1.18* |
| Delaware | 1.16* | .99 | .91 | 1.70* | .86 | .98 | 1.14 | 1.44* | 1.84* | .65* | 1.44* |
| Florida | 1.15* | .76* | .98 | .94 | 1.18* | .89 | 1.07 | 1.17* | .69* | .85* | 1.11 |
| Georgia | .94 | .96 | 1.05 | .98 | 1.08 | .95 | .56* | .66* | .74* | .81* | .69* |
| Idaho | .97 | 1.05 | .99 | .85* | 1.11 | 1.09 | 1.16* | .90 | .83* | .77* | 1.48* |
| Illinois | 1.12 | .96 | .97 | .73* | .95 | .94 | .86 | .62* | 1.51* | 1.09 | .83* |
| Indiana | 1.09 | .94 | .98 | .95 | .84* | .82* | 1.16* | .86 | .87 | 1.01 | .87 |
| Iowa | 1.03 | .93 | .96 | 1.12 | .83* | .92 | 1.18* | .83* | 1.11 | 1.17* | .96 |
| Kansas | .97 | .84* | 1.12 | 1.05 | .94 | 1.09 | .83* | .41* | 2.81* | .91 | .85* |
| Kentucky | .77* | 1.49* | .93 | .95 | .86 | .93 | .60* | .93 | .65* | .93 | .90 |
| Louisiana | .91 | 1.00 | 1.13 | 1.34* | .96 | 1.15* | 1.11 | 1.18* | .61* | .71* | .88 |
| Maine | .94 | .99 | 1.01 | .83* | .93 | .97 | 1.03 | 1.05 | .93 | 1.10 | 1.58* |
| Maryland | .95 | 1.00 | .97 | 1.24* | .88 | .87 | .91 | .86 | .93 | .82* | 1.45* |
| Massachusetts | 1.05 | .82* | 1.15* | .82* | 1.18* | .90 | 1.37* | .63* | .88 | .92 | .66* |
| Michigan | .87 | .97 | 1.07 | .93 | 1.21* | .77* | 1.50* | 1.02 | .77* | 1.22* | 1.14 |
| Minnesota | 1.02 | 1.06 | .92 | 1.07 | .83* | .93 | 1.31* | .85 | .91 | 1.10 | 1.25* |
| Mississippi | .93 | 1.12 | 1.00 | .90 | .99 | 1.06 | .54* | .74* | .94 | .75* | .86 |
| Missouri | .99 | .97 | .97 | .84* | .88 | .97 | .60* | 2.07* | .98 | .99 | .87 |
| Montana | 1.08 | .99 | .96 | 1.05 | 1.12 | 1.16 | .96 | 1.20* | .56* | 1.17* | 1.00 |

| | 1913 | 1918 | 1924 | 1929 | 1939 | 1942 | 1947 | 1952 | 1957 | 1962 | 1965 |
|---|---|---|---|---|---|---|---|---|---|---|---|
| Nebraska | .80* | .98 | .75* | .79* | .71* | 1.05 | .93 | .89 | .87 | .90 | 1.00 |
| Nevada | 1.22* | .86 | 1.53* | 1.20* | 1.08 | 1.16* | 1.20* | 1.08 | 1.03 | 1.07 | .96 |
| New Hampshire | .88 | 1.36* | .98 | 1.14 | 1.06 | 1.06 | .89 | .84* | 1.08 | .88 | .94 |
| New Jersey | 1.14 | 1.07 | .94 | 1.02 | .75* | .95 | 1.16* | .80* | .74* | .86 | .93 |
| New Mexico | .95 | 1.30* | 1.07 | 1.29* | .98 | 1.19* | 1.30* | 1.01 | 1.18* | .93 | 1.08 |
| New York | .94 | .96 | 1.07 | .93 | 1.28* | 1.00 | .90 | .80* | 1.05 | 1.05 | 1.00 |
| North Carolina | .68* | .83* | 1.02 | .97 | .72* | 1.00 | 1.06 | 1.16* | .80* | 1.00 | 1.03 |
| North Dakota | 1.20* | .94 | 1.10 | .92 | .84* | 1.15* | .96 | 1.29* | .95 | 1.06 | 1.05 |
| Ohio | .77* | .98 | .63* | .68* | 1.33* | .94 | .78* | .88 | .98 | .86 | .93 |
| Oklahoma | .88 | 1.23* | .79* | .89 | 1.22* | .96 | 1.13 | 1.24* | .97 | .94 | 1.02 |
| Oregon | .81* | .98 | 1.23* | 1.13 | .98 | 1.21* | .91 | 1.31* | .87 | 1.10 | .99 |
| Pennsylvania | .88 | .72* | 1.09 | .77* | 1.46* | .83* | .76* | .91 | .97 | .95 | 1.00 |
| Rhode Island | 1.03 | .88 | .84* | .99 | 1.11 | .71* | 1.54* | .71* | .99 | 1.05 | 1.09 |
| South Carolina | .65* | .78* | .95 | 1.04 | .69* | 1.05 | 1.08 | .95 | .89 | .92 | .98 |
| South Dakota | 1.05 | 1.03 | .96 | 1.08 | .85* | 1.12 | .86 | 1.01 | 1.02 | 1.06 | 1.01 |
| Tennessee | .91 | .99 | .71* | 1.39* | .60* | .90 | .93 | .96 | .91 | 1.01 | .99 |
| Texas | .80* | 1.05 | .87 | .89 | .81* | .83 | .83* | 1.03 | .94 | .92 | .96 |
| Utah | 1.08 | 1.18* | 1.00 | .90 | 1.43* | .99 | 1.05 | .87 | .92 | 1.18* | 1.17* |
| Vermont | 1.39* | 1.17* | .83* | 1.90* | .77* | 1.09 | .91 | .82* | 1.30* | 1.30* | .87 |
| Virginia | .90 | .95 | 1.06 | .82* | .66* | .99 | 1.08 | .86 | .98 | .83* | 1.05 |
| Washington | .77* | .98 | 1.30* | .97 | 1.37* | .89 | 1.59* | .90 | 1.05 | 1.06 | .95 |
| West Virginia | .74* | .83* | .95 | .85* | 1.14 | 1.16* | .79* | 1.20* | .72* | 1.18* | .95 |
| Wisconsin | 1.26* | .91 | .84* | .90 | .92 | 1.14 | .87 | 1.02 | .88 | 1.05 | 1.13 |
| Wyoming | 1.03 | 1.29* | 1.15* | 1.27* | 1.11 | 1.03 | .80* | 1.43* | 1.13 | 1.13 | 1.10 |

*An asterisk indicates that actual expenditures deviate from estimated expenditures by at least 15 per cent.

NOTE: Expenditures of each year are estimated on basis of expenditures of the most recent previous year reported here. Expenditures for 1913 are estimated on the basis of expenditures in 1903.

its general sales tax prior to its take-off. However, since 1929, most spurts have occurred without the stimulus of new taxes, and many states adopted major tax additions without experiencing a subsequent take-off in expenditures.

The ratios of Table III–8 permit the identification of the states that have been most and least erratic in their spending decisions throughout the twentieth century. Five states have shown only two instances of a marked spurt or lag with respect to the prevailing rates of change in expenditures (Maine, Minnesota, New Hampshire, New York, and Wisconsin); and one state (South Dakota) shows only one such instance. These states have increased their expenditures most in keeping with the nation-wide averages. The states that have been most erratic with respect to nation-wide rates of change include three states with six instances of marked spurt or lag (Alabama, Delaware, and Florida), one state with seven (Massachusetts), and two states with eight such instances (Vermont and West Virginia).

No simple explanation is apparent for the states that have increased their expenditures either in keeping or at odds with the national rates of change. The group of erratic states comes entirely from southern, border, or New England regions; but these regions exhibit no basic historical traits that clarify this particular spending pattern. Moreover, New England contributes two members to the states showing the least variations from prevailing rates of change. Each group of states includes both wealthy and poor economies and both urban-industrial and rural populations. Thus, there is no apparent economic difference between them. Likewise, the groups show no marked political differences. Each exhibits predominantly one-party states (both Republican and Democratic), plus competitive two-party states.

The techniques of comparative case studies may have much to offer for the explanation of state expenditures that do not fit prevailing patterns. Chapter VIII of this book returns to the data provided by the ratios of actual to estimated expenditures and discusses particular happenings in several states which shed light on their deviant scores.

## SUMMARY

This chapter has described the power and limitations of previous expenditures with respect to the current spending of American state governments. It finds a prominent stability in the relative positions of states' spending throughout the twentieth century. In periods of three to five years, there seems to be virtually no change in the relative positions of each state's expenditures. While the past seems to exert great influence over the present decisions of state budget-makers, however, state spending has changed greatly during the 62 years between 1903 and 1965. Without correcting for inflation, average state spending per capita increased 102 times!

How has the great increase in state expenditures existed along with the close relationships between past and present levels of spending for each state? The evidence suggests that during most periods all states have benefited from increases in spending without experiencing great changes in their relative positions. The explanations of changes experienced by all states in common will be the subject of Chapter V; that discussion will highlight the Great Depression, the war years, and the years following World War II and the Korean Conflict as occasions for changes in the spending of all states. But these influences have been general; they have had little differential effect upon rates of change in individual states.

One of the phenomena that has helped states maintain their spending positions relative to one another is their tendency to fluctuate between periods of relative increase and periods of stability or relative decline in spending. Individual states appear to increase their spending in spurts, and then hold to new positions. In an attempt to discern patterns of changes in state government spending, Chapter IV correlates measures of expenditure change with several indicators of governmental, political, and economic characteristics. After Chapter V considers the influence of factors that have had across-the-board influence on the expenditures of most states, Chapter VI returns to the subject of interstate variations in expenditure change; it considers the influence of regional norms on state spending.

## CHAPTER IV

# Governmental, Political, and Socio-economic Characteristics and State Government Expenditures

THIS CHAPTER BEGINS with the findings of Chapter III, which show the primacy of previous expenditures in the budget processes of American state governments. It tests the relative degrees of association among current expenditures, previous expenditures, and 46 other likely correlates of current expenditures. Aside from previous expenditures, the likely correlates of current expenditures include measures of three categories of state characteristics:

(1) Economic and social characteristics of personal well-being, industrialization, urbanization, taxable resources, education levels, and the incidence of ethnic minorities;

(2) Political characteristics of voter turnout, party strength, party competition, equity of urban-rural apportionment in the state legislature, and levels of activism and professionalism in the legislature;

(3) Governmental characteristics of federal aids, taxes, state-local financial relationships, and the nature of the state bureaucracy.

Finding that previous expenditure retains its primacy of association as suggested in preceding pages, this chapter then employs previous expenditure as a control variable and measures the partial relationships that exist between current expenditures and the other likely influences. Finally, it reexamines each of the 46 likely influences regarding their relationships with measures of change in expenditures. With a series of correlation and regression analyses, this chapter attempts to define the ways in which components of state government, state politics, economics, and society come to bear on the decisions of budget-makers.

The literature on government expenditures provides some ambiguous clues about the relationships to be expected between state expenditures and the socio-economic correlates that are tested here. Many publications that are relevant deal with the combination of state and local government expenditures for each state. In general, the findings show that state plus local government expenditures per capita are likely to be high where economic indicators show high levels of personal well-being, industrialization, urbanization, and education.[1] Yet it is not certain that similar findings prevail in the case of state government expenditures alone. While local officials tend to be limited in their taxing powers by virtue of their constitutionally enforced reliance on the real property tax, state authorities enjoy access to a wider range of taxes, and they can impose their taxes on the full breadth of the state economy. There are many local governments (especially rural counties) in poor states that find it virtually impossible to support a minimum service program on the real property tax base that is available to their direct action.[2] Moreover, state officials have enjoyed access to greater amounts of direct federal aid than have local authorities. During 1962, state governments received $7,108 million from federal sources, while local governments received only $763 million. The federal contribution amounted to 22.8 per cent of the states' general revenue, but only 1.9 per cent of local governments' general revenue.[3] As a result of these conditions, state officials may have greater flexibility in the face of economic adversity, and they may be less dependent than local officials on the magnitude of financial resources. In localities where the people and their local governments are poor, an ab-

---

[1]See, for example, Thomas R. Dye, *Politics, Economics, and the Public: Policy Outcomes in the American States* (Chicago: Rand McNally & Co., 1966); Richard E. Dawson and James A. Robinson, "Interparty Competition, Economic Variables, and Welfare Politics in the American States," *Journal of Politics,* 25 (May 1963): 265–89; Richard Hofferbert, "The Relation between Public Policy and Some Structural and Environmental Variables in the American States," *American Political Science Review,* 60 (March 1966): 73–82; Solomon Fabricant, *The Trend of Government Activity in the United States since 1900* (New York: National Bureau of Economic Research, 1952); Glenn W. Fisher, "Interstate Variation in State and Local Government Expenditures," *National Tax Journal,* 17 (March 1964): 57–84; and Seymour Sachs and Robert Harris, "The Determinants of State and Local Government Expenditures and Intergovernmental Flow of Funds," *National Tax Journal,* 17 (March 1964): 75–85.

[2]Dick Netzer, *Economics of the Property Tax* (Washington: Brookings Institution, 1965), p. 6.

[3]U.S. Bureau of the Census, *Census of Governments, 1962: Compendium of Government Finances* (Washington: U.S. Government Printing Office), p. 28.

normal proportion of service responsibilities may flow to the agencies of the state (as opposed to local) governments. Although the aggregate of resources may be lowest in underdeveloped economies, state governments may actually spend most under conditions of economic underdevelopment.

Measures of ethnicity have served in the analysis of local government activity as indicators of interest groups that bring pressure to bear on municipal officials for improved services.[4] Although this study tests the incidence of non-whites and "foreign stock" as correlates of state spending, it seems likely that they will fail to show strong relationship with the dependent variables. The incidence of non-whites may have varying effect on state officials in both the North and the South; when the 48 states make up the universe of analysis, the coefficient of simple correlation between percentage non-white and state spending is not likely to reflect a consistent pattern of relationship. Even in the absence of regional differences in the political status of non-whites, the concept of ethnicity would appear to be weaker at the state level of government than in the localities. States are more heterogeneous than communities; while ethnic organizations might have sufficient strength to affect the decisions of local government officials, they may not have sufficient numbers in enough communities to influence officials over the larger domain of the state.

It is reasonable to expect that political characteristics influence the level of state spending. One of the topics that politicians dispute most intensely is the nature of government expenditures. But the available research does not clearly indicate the impact on state spending from political characteristics. Studies of party competition and voter turnout show positive relationships among the degree of two-party competition for state offices, the level of voter turnout, and the *combined expenditures of state and local governments*. Studies of the activism and professionalism of legislators find similar positive relationships between these characteristics and public policies; however, studies of legislative districting show no relationship between the equity of apportionment with respect to urban and rural voters and the level of state and local government activities.[5] States may have similar political characteristics, but a different

[4]See, for example, John H. Kessel, "Governmental Structure and Political Environment: A Statistical Note about American Cities," *American Political Science Review*, 56 (September 1962): 615–20.
[5]See Dye, "Politics"; Dawson and Robinson, "Interparty Competition"; Hofferbert, "Relation"; and John G. Grumm, "Structure and Policy in the Legislature" (paper presented at a meeting of the Southwestern Social Science Association, March 1967).

set of governmental outcomes. Politicians may tolerate identical procedures for different programmatic reasons; like players in a game, they
might agree on the rules but strive for different results. In order to examine the relationship between state political characteristics and state
government expenditures, this chapter considers the political measures of
party strength and party competition, voter turnout, state legislative apportionment, legislative activity, and the professionalism of the legislature with respect to salaries, supporting facilities, and length of session.

Indicators of federal aid, state taxation, state-local financial relationships, and state government employees measure characteristics of the
state government that appear critical to the decisions of state budget-
makers. It is expected that the proportion of state revenue received from
the federal government, the proportion of personal income paid by residents in state taxes, the per capita amounts of revenue received by the
state under each of three major taxes, and the percentage of revenue
received from specific taxes will show positive relationships with state
expenditures per capita. Briefly stated, the general hypothesis is that
expenditures will be high where they are supported by a generous provision of federal grants, high citizen tax effort, and productive tax
systems. The measures of taxes are not merely the revenue side of expenditures. The independent variable that measures total state taxes is
defined in a way that guards against the necessary finding that high tax
receipts correspond with high expenditures. The tax indicator shows the
proportion of residents' personal income that is paid in state taxes.
Thus, it reflects the tax *effort* put forth by citizens, and permits the assessment of the relationship between their effort and the per capita level of
state expenditures. While it is expected that high tax effort will correspond with high expenditures per capita, it is not unlikely that some states
will show higher levels of expenditure than are suggested by their citizens'
tax effort; the residents of wealthy states may make much greater tax
payments than residents of poorer states, while still showing lower
measures of tax effort.

Another major hypothesis of this chapter asserts that state expenditures per capita are high where the state has assumed a higher-than-
average share of state and local government financial responsibilities.
While the high spending obligations of a state that has a large share of
service responsibilities (that are carried by local governments in other
states) may appear patently obvious to some readers, there is nothing
automatic about a "centralized" state being a high-spending state. If the
state has acquired its share of financial responsibilities because anti-
spending doctrines prevail at the local level, similar doctrines might also

hold down the level of spending by state agencies. It is also expected that positive relationships exist among the size of a state's bureaucracy (relative to population), the average salary of state employees, and current expenditures per capita. Presumably, these measures of the state bureaucracy reflect the size and past success of an interest group (state employees) that works in favor of high spending. The measure of the bureaucracy's size may also reflect the magnitude of state services and their demands on the state budget. Yet there is no necessary relationship among the number of state employees, the level of their salaries, and the size of the state budget. Some states may employ an excessive number of workers for the benefits that such employment provides to the well-being of individuals or the ruling political party. Patronage staffs may show generally low salaries as personnel funds are spread to a maximum number of jobs. When the motivations supporting large staffs are not related to the goals of excellence in public services, there may be no association between large employment and expenditures per capita.

## TECHNIQUES

The measures of state expenditures employed here are similar to those used in Chapter III. *Current expenditures* are general expenditures per capita in 1962. The year 1962 is considered current because a large number of potentially significant independent variables are available for that year in the *Census of Governments*. The principal measures of expenditure change are the 1962-1965 percentage change in general expenditures per capita and the 1962–1965 change in absolute dollars of general expenditures per capita. In each analysis there are measures of total expenditures and of expenditures for the major fields of public service.

The independent variables are 46 measures of governmental, political, economic, and social characteristics of the American states which seem capable of exerting influence upon the level of current state government spending or changes in spending. The full title and source of each independent variable is reported in the Appendix (see pp. 156–59).

As noted in Chapter I, both political and governmental characteristics measure aspects of state political systems. The principal distinctions between the two categories are: The political measures refer to electoral, partisan, and legislative phenomena that deal with the access of citizens to government decisions; these are considered by other authors as measures of the state political system. The governmental measures, which appear to be newly introduced in this study, assess aspects of state taxation, federal aid, state-local financial relations, and the state bureaucracy.

The analysis proceedes in four stages. First, coefficients of simple correlation indicate the degree of correspondence between 1962 expenditures per capita and each of the independent variables. On the basis of these data, there is a preliminary discussion of the findings in relation to the ambiguous expectations derived from existing literature, as discussed above. Second, coefficients of partial correlation serve to assess the relative "independence" of relationships between current expenditures and the 46 variables, while controlling for the level of previous expenditures. This test will successively determine: (1) if previous expenditures show a significant relationship to current expenditures while controlling for each of the other variables; and (2) if each of the other variables shows a significant relationship to current expenditures while controlling for previous expenditures. Since previous expenditures play such a direct role in the deliberations of budget-makers, it is expected that this will remain the most powerful of the independent variables, while controlling for all others. Yet certain of the other variables are strong enough to show significant relationships to current spending while taking account of previous spending. Third, a step-wise regression technique selects the most powerful independent variables. A step-wise program[6] first selects the independent variable that shows the strongest coefficient of simple correlation with the dependent variable. The coefficient of multiple determination ($R^2$) associated with this variable indicates the percentage of interstate variation in spending that is explained by this independent variable alone. In subsequent steps, the program selects the variables that, when added to the regression formula, account for the greatest proportion of still unexplained variation in spending. With the addition of each independent variable to the formula, the proportion of spending that is explained increases; but after the inclusion of the most powerful independent variables, subsequent additions provide little further statistical explanation of variations in spending. The tables below stop reporting the addition of further independent variables when they fail to add 5 per cent to the existing coefficient of multiple determination.[7] Finally,

[6]"Step-Wise Regression: BMD02R," *Biomedical Computer Programs* (Los Angeles: University of California Health Sciences Computing Facility, 1965), pp. 233–57.

[7]While step-wise regression is invaluable in demonstrating the amount of interstate variation that certain independent variables explain, it does not test for the independence of the variable having the strongest coefficient of simple correlation with spending. Yet, as Table IV–3 shows, the variable chosen first in the case of current spending (the level of previous spending) does show a relationship with the dependent variable that is independent with respect to other correlates.

these tests are repeated with measures of expenditure change as the dependent variables. In this way, it can be determined if the factors associated with current levels of spending show similar relationships with measures of change in spending.

## FINDINGS: CURRENT EXPENDITURES

As expected, there are positive relationships between current expenditures and measures of federal aid, taxation, the centralization of state-local financial relationships, state employees, and their average salaries. State spending per capita seems to be supported by a high incidence of federal aid among state revenues, by taxes that demand a high percentage of citizens' personal income, by a large and well-paid bureaucracy, and by state financial responsibility for a relatively high proportion of state-local activities. Table IV–1 reports coefficients of simple correlation between each of the independent variables and total state government expenditures per capita.

The relationships between economic characteristics and state government expenditures tend to be negative. This finding stands in marked contrast to the findings obtained from analysis of the combination of state and local government spending. The studies of Fabricant, Fisher, and Sachs and Harris, among economists, and the studies of Dye, Daw-

TABLE IV–1

Coefficients of Simple Correlation between Independent Variables
and Total State Government Expenditures per Capita, 1962

|  | *Total Expenditures/Capita* |
| --- | --- |
| SOCIO-ECONOMIC MEASURES | |
| personal income (2)[a] | —.26 |
| personal income per capita (3) | .14 |
| urbanization (4) | .08 |
| population (5) | —.32* |
| population growth (6) | .25 |
| labor force in manufacturing (7) | —.51* |
| value added by manufacturing per capita (8) | —.38* |
| adults with college education (9) | .36* |
| families with low income (10) | —.18 |
| population density (11) | —.30* |
| area (12) | .18 |
| non-agricultural labor force (13) | —.05 |
| non-white population (14) | —.19 |
| population foreign-born or of foreign or mixed parentage (15) | .03 |

## TABLE IV–1 (Continued)

|  | Total Expenditures/Capita |
|---|---|
| **POLITICAL MEASURES** | |
| voter turnout for U.S. Representative election (16) | .22 |
| voter turnout for gubernatorial election (17) | .23 |
| party competition in lower house (18)[b,c] | .09 |
| party competition in upper house (19)[b,c] | .18 |
| party competition in U.S. Representative election (20)[c] | —.04 |
| party competition in gubernatorial election (21)[c] | .17 |
| gubernatorial tenure (22) | .19 |
| legislative compensation (23) | —.22 |
| bills introduced per session (24) | —.12 |
| bills passed per session (25) | —.25 |
| length of legislative session (26) | —.14 |
| financial support of legislature (27) | .28* |
| S-P index of malapportionment (28) | —.17 |
| D-K index of malapportionment (29) | —.22 |
| D-E index of malapportionment (30) | —.03 |
| lower-house tenure (31)[b] | —.07 |
| upper-house tenure (32)[b] | .01 |
| number of legislators (33) | —.24 |
| **GOVERNMENTAL MEASURES** | |
| federal aid (34) | .40* |
| tax effort (35) | .55* |
| income tax per capita (36) | .25 |
| sales tax per capita (37) | .20 |
| excise tax per capita (38) | .35* |
| income tax as % of total taxes (39) | .50* |
| sales tax as % of total taxes (40) | .51* |
| excise tax as % of total taxes (41) | .39* |
| state % of state-local expenditures (42) | .54* |
| % of state-local revenues to state (43) | .46* |
| revenues from non-local sources (44) | .53* |
| local expenditures per capita (45) | .06 |
| salaries of state employees (46) | .29* |
| employees per population (47) | .68* |

*Significant at the .05 level.

[a]Numbers in parentheses refer to the numbered variables identified in the Appendix, pp. 156–59.

[b]These measures of interparty competition in state legislatures are not directly relevant to the non-partisan legislatures of Nebraska and Minnesota. In order to obtain meaningful data for these states, scores obtained from a comparable measurement of competition for the governor's office were inserted as their scores for competition in the legislature. In order to cope with Nebraska's unicameral legislature, its competition score was inserted into both upper- and lower-house measures.

[c]All the measures of party competition actually measure the strength of the dominant party in state politics. For a measure of competitiveness *per se*, the reader might consider using the inverse of this variable. See Appendix, p. 157.

son and Robinson, and Hofferbert,[8] among political scientists, all find strong positive relationships between economic indicators (similar to those used here) and the aggregate spending per capita of state and local governments. Apparently, the level of economic resources that work to support (or retard) all state and local spending within a state has a different impact upon the spending of state agencies alone. It is states with low levels of population, density, and industrialization which show the highest levels of state government spending. The variable of per capita personal income (which shows a $+.60$ correlation coefficient with the *combination* of state and local spending per capita) fails to show a significant relationship with state government spending.

Why do measures of population and industrialization stand in inverse relationships with state government expenditures? If one views the measures of economic characteristics solely as measures of *resources,* the answer does not come quickly. It is difficult to discern how an abundance of resources leads to low expenditures by state governments. But the economic measures reflect *needs* as well as resources, and the needs of localities in states scoring low in population and industrialization suggest the linkage between low economic scores and a high level of state government spending.

Low economic resources appear to effect relatively high state government expenditures because of the economy's impact on the spending of local governments.[9] When a state's population is small and non-industrial, there are a number of local governments (especially rural counties) that are hard-pressed to support minimal service needs with their own resources. Part of the local governments' problems in such states rests on their enforced reliance on a tax base that is dependent upon local resources. State constitutions generally restrict local governments to the tax on locally situated real property. During the depression, especially, and since the depression in rural, non-industrial states, the real property tax has been vulnerable in the face of low property values.[10]

State governments have the capacity to assist with the needs of local authorities that are under low-resource conditions. The states have legal access to the economic resources within their larger jurisdiction; they

[8]See their works cited in note 1.

[9]The coefficient of simple correlation between per capita personal income and local government expenditures per capita is .82.

[10]See Netzer, *Economics of the Property Tax,* p. 6. The economic dependence of the real property tax is evidenced by the strong positive relationship ($r = .55$) between per capita personal income and state and local property tax collections per capita in 1962; in contrast, state and local per capita collections in personal income and general sales taxes (largely collected at the state level) showed insignificant correlation coefficients with per capita personal income ($r = .25; r = -.01$).

benefit from a larger and more generous selection of federal aids; and they have a more varied taxing network to extract revenue from available resources. The state levies on personal income, general sales, and taxed commodities have remained more productive in the face of depressed economic conditions than has the local property tax. Chapter V shows that the state share of state and local government finances increased during the 1932–1940 depression period from 36 to 48 per cent of the total. Since the 1930's, the centralization of state-local finances has been a characteristic of states having low levels of urbanization, industrialization, and personal income.[11] Because of the more favorable revenue positions of state governments, they tend to receive a larger share of state-local financial responsibilities under low-resources conditions.

There is virtually no association between state scores on expenditures per capita and the measures of political characteristics considered here. While this finding differs in detail from those resulting from an analysis of state plus local government expenditures, the basic findings appear similar. The research of Dye, Hofferbert, and Dawson and Robinson shows positive simple relationships among voter turnout, party competition, and the level of combined state and local government expenditures. Yet their findings disappear when they control for the influence of economic resources on both political characteristics and expenditures. These authors suggest that there is little association between state and local government expenditures and political characteristics that is not, basically, an appearance generated by the common influence of economic resources on both political characteristics and the combined expenditures of state and local governments. The present data also find no meaningful association between political characteristics and state government spending.

A brief examination of the highest and lowest spending states serves to dramatize the lack of political uniformities among states at various spending levels. Table IV–2 shows the five highest- and five lowest-spending states of 1962. The high-spending states include those showing one-party Democratic and Republican dominance (Louisiana and Vermont) and intense two-party competition (Nevada and Wyoming). Louisiana shows the low voter turnout that characterizes the South, while the mountain states show the high turnout typical of their region. And public officials in Louisiana flavor their activities with flamboyance and scandal, while Vermonters do their public business with Yankee reserve and ap-

---

[11] The coefficient of simple correlation between per capita personal income and the percentage of state and local revenue allocated to the state is —.49; and the coefficient between per capita personal income and the percentage of state and local revenue from non-local sources is —.54.

TABLE IV–2

States Showing Highest and Lowest Total Spending per Capita, 1962

|  | *Total Expenditures/Capita* |
|---|---|
| Wyoming | $283.69 |
| Nevada | 277.06 |
| Vermont | 255.10 |
| Louisiana | 251.74 |
| Washington | 249.62 |
| Florida | 135.79 |
| Illinois | 131.33 |
| Ohio | 130.34 |
| Nebraska | 125.49 |
| New Jersey | 110.47 |

parent honesty. Sharp differences also exist in the politics of the low-spending states. Florida's Democratic background contrasts with the Republican tendencies in the state politics of Ohio, Illinois, and Nebraska.

The lack of significant correlation coefficients between state government spending and the measures of voter turnout, party strength, inter-party competition, and the nature of the legislature does not signify a lack of political influence over state budget-makers. Findings only show that certain readily measured political characteristics do not vary from state to state in the same manner as expenditures. Expenditures result from a process that is intimately involved with politics, and the aspirations, alliances, and skills of politicians make themselves felt in budgeting. Chapter VIII describes several instances when the desires and strengths of political leaders and the policy-inclinations of large political groups seem to have had telling influence during critical periods in the recent histories of individual states' budgets.

While it is apparent that a number of governmental and economic characteristics show significant simple relationships with current spending per capita, the question lingers whether these relationships remain in the face of strong linkages between previous and present expenditures. The data of Table IV–3 help to answer this question; they show coefficients of partial correlation between current expenditures, previous expenditures, and each of the other independent variables. These coefficients

TABLE IV–3

Coefficients of Partial Correlation between Current Total State
Expenditures per Capita and Previous Expenditures, and between Current Total
State Expenditures per Capita and Each of the Remaining Independent Variables

|  | *Previous Expenditures*[a] | *Independent Variables*[b] |
|---|---|---|
| SOCIO-ECONOMIC MEASURES |  |  |
| personal income (2)[c] | .85* | —.19 |
| personal income per capita (3) | .86* | .24 |
| urbanization (4) | .88* | —.41* |
| population (5) | .84* | —.21 |
| population growth (6) | .85* | —.26 |
| labor force in manufacturing (7) | .80* | —.20 |
| value added by manufacturing per capita (8) | .84* | —.29* |
| adults with college education (9) | .84* | —.28* |
| families with low income (10) | .85* | .21 |
| population density (11) | .85* | —.31* |
| area (12) | .85* | .03 |
| non-agricultural labor force (13) | .86* | —.26 |
| non-white population (14) | .85* | —.11 |
| population foreign-born or of foreign or mixed parentage (15) | .85* | —.15 |
| POLITICAL MEASURES |  |  |
| voter turnout for U.S. Representative election (16) | .84* | .04 |
| voter turnout for gubernatorial election (17) | .84* | .11 |
| party competition in lower house (18)[d,e] | .85* | .09 |
| party competition in upper house (19)[d,e] | .86* | .24 |
| party competition in U.S. Representative election (20)[e] | .85* | —.03 |
| party competition in gubernatorial election (21)[e] | .85* | .12 |
| gubernatorial tenure (22) | .85* | —.10 |
| legislative compensation (23) | .85* | —.19 |
| bills introduced per session (24) | .85* | —.17 |
| bills passed per session (25) | .86* | —.37* |
| length of legislative session (26) | .85* | .02 |
| financial support of legislature (27) | .86* | .22 |
| S-P index of malapportionment (28) | .85* | .05 |
| D-K index of malapportionment (29) | .85* | .23 |
| D-E index of malapportionment (30) | .85* | .09 |
| lower-house tenure (31)[d] | .85* | —.02 |
| upper-house tenure (32)[d] | .85* | —.07 |
| number of legislators (33) | .86* | —.29* |

TABLE IV–3 (Contnued)

|  | Previous Expenditures[a] | Independent Variables[b] |
|---|---|---|
| GOVERNMENTAL MEASURES | | |
| federal aid (34) | .84* | .34* |
| tax effort (35) | .82* | .42* |
| income tax per capita (36) | .85* | .18 |
| sales tax per capita (37) | .85* | .06 |
| excise tax per capita (38) | .83* | .07 |
| income tax as % of total taxes (39) | .85* | .29* |
| sales tax as % of total taxes (40) | .85* | .33* |
| excise tax as % of total taxes (41) | .84* | .37* |
| state % of state-local expenditures (42) | .84* | .48* |
| % of state-local revenues to state (43) | .84* | .41* |
| revenues from non-local sources (44) | .83* | .43* |
| local expenditures per capita (45) | .83* | .15 |
| salaries of state employees (46) | .84* | .05 |
| employees per population (47) | .76* | .42* |

*Significant at the .05 level.

[a]Coefficients of partial correlation in this column indicate the relationships of previous expenditures to current expenditures, while controlling for the effects of the corresponding independent variables.

[b]Coefficients of partial correlation in this column indicate the relationships of the corresponding independent variables to current expenditures, while controlling for the effects of previous expenditures.

[c]See note a in Table IV–1.

[d]See note b in Table IV–1.

[e]See note c in Table IV–1.

show the continuing dominance of previous expenditures. When each of the other independent variables is considered along with past spending, the previous levels of spending continue to show relationships in the magnitude of +.85 with current spending. Yet a number of the independent variables also show significant relationships with current spending when considered along with previous spending.

The basic nature of relationships among current spending, governmental characteristics, and economics—while controlling for previous spending—differs little from the simple relationships described above. There are significant positive partial relationships between current spending and federal aid, tax effort, the size of the state bureaucracy, and the centralization of state-local finances; and there are significant negative partial relationships between current expenditures and the economic characteristics of urbanization, industrialization, and population density. Also, as in the case with simple relationships, there is no significant partial association between current spending and the readily measured political characteristics of party strength, interparty competition, voter turnout, or the nature of legislative apportionment. However, two measures of legislative size and activism show significant negative partial relationships with spending. Although these findings alone suggest that the size and activity of legislative bodies work against high state spending, the findings receive little support from the coefficients associated with other indicators of legislative characteristics.

The coefficients of partial correlation testify both to the power and to the limitations of previous expenditures with respect to current state expenditures. Past spending is clearly the independent variable related most directly to current spending. This finding squares with the observations of political scientists and economists who have studied decision-making in government budgeting: participants seem to consider no single factor in making their decisions as frequently as they consult the magnitude of previous expenditures.[12] Yet previous spending is not the only salient influence. Several independent variables show significant relationships with current spending while controlling for previous spending; and as a concept, previous spending does not contain within itself the stimuli of changes in expenditures. The next section of this chapter shows that the level of previous spending *does not* exert pervasive influence over the increments of change in expenditures.

While the coefficients of partial correlation establish the primacy of previous expenditures among the independent variables that have influence on current expenditures, they do not clearly indicate what independent variables have secondary importance. The sheer magnitude of partial correlation coefficients is little help because they do not control for relationships among all of the independent variables. For example, depending upon the relationships of the *percentage employed in manufacturing* and the *state percentage of state-local expenditures* to the other independent variables, either of these variables could show the stronger independent relationship to current expenditures. A step-wise regression program offers a means of showing the importance of relationships between a dependent variable (current spending per capita) and a large number of independent variables. After a step-wise program identifies the independent variable that shows the strongest simple relationship with a dependent variable, it searches among the available correlates for one

[12]See Charles E. Lindblom, "Decision-Making in Taxation and Expenditure," in National Bureau of Economic Research, *Public Finances: Needs, Sources and Utilization* (Princeton, N.J.: Princeton University Press, 1961), pp. 295–336; Aaron Wildavsky, *The Politics of the Budgetary Process* (Boston: Little, Brown & Co., 1964); and Thomas J. Anton, *The Politics of State Expenditure in Illinois* (Urbana: University of Illinois Press, 1966).

that will add the greatest amount of explanatory power to the simple relationship already established. In subsequent steps, the program continues to select variables that will add most to the explanation of a dependent variable. Table IV–4 shows the results of a step-wise program applied to current spending per capita and the list of 46 independent variables considered in this chapter.

The results of step-wise regression point to governmental characteristics as having the greatest impact on the level of state government spending. As expected, the most powerful independent variable is previous spending; by itself, this factor accounts for 72 per cent of the interstate variation in 1962 spending per capita. Second in importance is the percentage of state and local expenditures made by state agencies; together with previous spending, this item increases the statistical explanation to 79 per cent of the interstate variation. Finally, the addition of local government expenditures per capita increases the level of explanation to 95 per cent of the interstate variation.

The importance of local government spending as a correlate of state spending does not appear in the simple or partial correlation coefficients reported above; yet it reveals its importance in a regression analysis with the two variables of previous spending and the state percentage of state-local expenditures. The regression coefficient of local government expenditures per capita is positive, indicating that among states with comparable levels of previous spending and the centralization of state-local financing, there is a tendency for high scores in state and local government spending to occur together. In such states, the historical factors that have resulted in high (or low) levels of spending at the local level appear to have operated in similar fashion at the state level.

In most cases, the correlates of current spending according to major field of service resemble the correlates of total spending. However, the

TABLE IV–4

Coefficients of Multiple Determination
Associated with the Most Powerful Independent Variables,
as Determined by Step-wise Regression

| Dependent Variable: Total State Government Expenditures per Capita, 1962 | |
| --- | --- |
| *Variables Added* | $R^2$ |
| Previous expenditures (1957) | .72 |
| State % of state-local expenditures | .79 |
| Local expenditures per capita | .95 |

coefficients of Table IV–5, when compared to those of Table IV–1, show some deviations that reflect specific factors working on budgets of individual agencies. Spending for education and welfare, for example, shows fewer relationships with political characteristics than spending for other fields of service. Perhaps professional administrators in charge of state welfare and educational agencies are more isolated than other agencies' officials from the influence of parties and elected officials. In the case of public welfare programs, federal aids for the categorical assistance programs (aid for the aged, the blind, the disabled, and dependent children) may remove the welfare sector from the purview of elected officials. Yet the insignificant relationship between federal aid and welfare spending does not support such a view ($r = +.12$). Welfare spending may not be isolated from politics as much as it is isolated from a patterned relationship with the components of the political process which are measured here. Compared to other programs, public welfare may vary with ideological habits within each state, and these ideological phenomena may themselves vary independently from the economic, political, or governmental characteristics that are cited in this chapter. More than in other fields, spending for health and hospitals, public safety, and general government shows positive relationships to several measures of state economic characteristics. These services account for a relatively small portion of state expenditures (14 per cent in 1962), and their priorities may be lower than for such programs as education and highways. As a result, less wealthy states may be inclined to postpone or minimize spending for health and hospitals, public safety, and general government. Highways and natural resources are unique in showing strong positive relationships with the measure of federal aid, thus testifying to the importance of federal programs for primary, secondary, and interstate highways, and for conservation and agricultural extension activities. Highway spending also shows a strong positive relationship to the percentage of state taxes that are collected as excises. These findings may reflect the role of earmarked gasoline taxes in state highway financing; but the weak relationship between per capita excise taxes and per capita highway spending ($r = +.22$) serves to question this interpretation and to highlight the need for more specialized research in the field of highway spending.

This study has concentrated on the examination of factors that affect the gross phenomenon of total state government expenditures per capita. It is evident that there remains much to be done in explaining interstate variations in spending in the major fields of services. In subsequent analyses, it may be necessary to develop specialized independent variables that take account of factors that affect budget-makers in particular service areas.

TABLE IV-5

Coefficients of Simple Correlation between Independent Variables
and State Government Expenditures per Capita, by Major Field, 1962

| | State Expenditures per Capita | | | | | | |
|---|---|---|---|---|---|---|---|
| | Education | Highways | Public Welfare | Health and Hospitals | Natural Resources | Public Safety | General Government |
| SOCIO-ECONOMIC MEASURES | | | | | | | |
| personal income (2)[a] | −.11 | −.41* | −.01 | .11 | −.37* | −.02 | −.07 |
| personal income/capita (3) | .00 | −.03 | −.11 | .44* | .07 | .63* | .46* |
| urbanization (4) | .03 | −.39* | .09 | .29* | −.30* | .26 | .28* |
| population (5) | −.12 | −.46* | −.02 | .12 | −.43* | −.10 | −.17 |
| population growth (6) | .33* | −.02 | −.05 | −.11 | .14 | .41* | .37* |
| labor force in manufacturing (7) | −.46* | −.42* | −.18 | .35* | −.49* | −.08 | −.25 |
| value added by manufacturing/capita (8) | −.33* | −.41* | −.14 | .40* | −.54* | .12 | −.08 |
| adults with college education (9) | .45* | .02 | .06 | .28* | .13 | .55* | .49* |
| families with low income (10) | −.04 | −.13 | .16 | −.38* | −.13 | −.59* | −.48* |
| population density (11) | −.37* | −.39* | −.08 | .48* | −.45* | .07 | .20 |
| area (12) | .36* | .12 | .07 | −.47* | .28* | .02 | .03 |
| non-agricultural labor force (13) | .06 | −.34* | .09 | .35* | −.33* | .28* | .30* |
| non-white population (14) | .07 | −.36* | .05 | −.09 | −.31* | −.32* | −.36* |
| population foreign-born or of foreign or mixed parentage (15) | −.25 | .05 | −.11 | .43* | .05 | .34* | .37* |
| POLITICAL MEASURES | | | | | | | |
| voter turnout for U.S. Representative election (16) | .01 | .29* | −.04 | .18 | .24 | .33* | .39* |
| voter turnout for gubernatorial election (17) | .10 | .20 | .11 | .12 | .17 | .25 | .27 |

TABLE IV-5 (Continued)

| | State Expenditures per Capita | | | | | | |
|---|---|---|---|---|---|---|---|
| | Education | Highways | Public Welfare | Health and Hospitals | Natural Resources | Public Safety | General Government |
| POLITICAL MEASURES (Cont.) | | | | | | | |
| party competition in lower house (18)[b,c] | −.02 | .11 | −.11 | .09 | .16 | .30* | .23 |
| party competition in upper house (19)[b,c] | −.01 | .23 | −.09 | .18 | .16 | .35* | .37* |
| party competition in U.S. Representative election (20)[c] | −.08 | .07 | −.20 | .10 | −.01 | .25 | .13 |
| party competition in gubernatorial election (21)[c] | .03 | .16 | .01 | .17 | .10 | .25 | .19 |
| gubernatorial tenure (22) | .07 | .09 | .11 | .24 | .05 | .30* | .24 |
| legislative compensation (23) | −.14 | −.39* | .04 | .32* | −.44* | .02 | −.11 |
| bills introduced per session (24) | −.11 | −.38* | .03 | .48* | −.33* | .04 | .14 |
| bills passed per session (25) | −.13 | −.45* | −.03 | .35* | −.28* | .04 | −.03 |
| length of legislative session (26) | −.16 | −.27 | .08 | .24 | −.33* | .11 | −.07 |
| financial support of legislature (27) | .25 | .38* | −.06 | −.36* | .48* | .06 | .12 |
| S-P index of malapportionment (28) | −.26 | .07 | −.16 | .03 | .03 | −.01 | .23 |
| D-K index of malapportionment (29) | −.29* | −.04 | .04 | −.08 | −.03 | −.29* | −.30* |
| D-E index of malapportionment (30) | −.27 | −.05 | .07 | .46* | −.15 | .20 | .12 |
| lower-house tenure (31) | .00 | .09 | −.17 | −.16 | .27 | .09 | .04 |
| upper-house tenure (32) | −.09 | −.02 | .12 | .16 | .18 | .16 | .20 |
| number of legislators (33) | −.40* | −.14 | .21 | .32* | .29* | −.16 | −.16 |
| GOVERNMENTAL MEASURES | | | | | | | |
| federal aid (34) | .19 | .65* | .12 | −.45* | .68* | .03 | .21 |
| tax effort (35) | .66* | .11 | .46* | −.08 | .19 | −.01 | .13 |
| income tax/capita (36) | .23 | −.03 | .03 | .46* | .04 | .34* | .28* |

TABLE IV-5 (Continued)

| | State Expenditures per Capita | | | | | | |
| | Education | Highways | Public Welfare | Health and Hospitals | Natural Resources | Public Safety | General Government |
|---|---|---|---|---|---|---|---|
| GOVERNMENTAL MEASURES (Cont.) | | | | | | | |
| sales tax/capita (37) | .38* | −.05 | .26 | −.28* | −.05 | −.05 | .00 |
| excise tax/capita (38) | .17 | .22 | −.18 | −.15 | .07 | .45* | .47* |
| income tax as % of total taxes (39) | .27 | .34* | −.02 | .26 | .25 | .33* | .30* |
| sales tax as % of total taxes (40) | .33* | .56* | −.04 | −.25 | .53* | .24 | .47* |
| excise tax as % of total taxes (41) | .11 | .74* | −.17 | .03 | .59* | .45* | .56* |
| state % of state-local expenditures (42) | .55* | .21 | .37* | −.12 | .20 | −.04 | .14 |
| % of state-local revenues to state (43) | .28* | .49* | .28* | −.15 | .37* | −.05 | .20 |
| revenues from non-local sources (44) | .60* | .24 | .32* | −.15 | .22 | .01 | .16 |
| local expenditures/capita (45) | −.14 | .16 | −.21 | .23 | .20 | .42* | .31* |
| salaries of state employees (46) | .16 | .10 | −.10 | .33* | .19 | .61* | .50* |
| employees per population (47) | .45* | .64* | .23 | .07 | .66* | .30* | .47* |
| 1957 expenditures, by field | .93* | .63* | .93* | .84* | .78* | .70* | .95* |

*Significant at the .05 level.
[a]See note a in Table IV–1.
[b]See note b in Table IV–1.
[c]See note c in Table IV–1.

## FINDINGS: CHANGES IN EXPENDITURES

The governmental and economic characteristics that show significant relationships with current spending tend to show similar relationships with the measures of expenditure change. The states showing a high score on 1962–1965 percentage or absolute increases in total spending per capita generally show a high incidence of federal aid, a centralization of state-local financial relationships, a large bureaucracy, productive taxes, and low levels of industrialization. However, the data of Table IV–6 show that these relationships tend to be weaker in magnitude than relationships between the same independent variables and the measure of current spending.

The political characteristics of American states seem to have greater impact on the increment of change in spending than on the level of current spending. The coefficients of Table IV–6 indicate that voter turnout and the strength of the governor's party show positive relationships with both measures of expenditure change. And the size of the legislature shows a significant inverse relationship with a measure of change in spending. Why do political characteristics show more of a relationship with changes in spending than the level of current spending? The reason may be that the level of current spending represents an accretion of many years' time when the influence of economic and governmental characteristics have prevailed. However, at the point of deciding upon the direction and size of change embodied in a new budget, the interest of the electorate and the strength of the majority party might be salient.

The step-wise regression analysis of expenditure change supports two principal findings: (1) the independent variables that are most directly associated with the measures of change include a mixture of political, economic, and governmental characteristics; and (2) the aggregate of important variables leaves unexplained much of the interstate variation in expenditure change. As shown in Table IV–7, each of these findings differs considerably from the findings associated with current expenditures. There (Table IV–4) it was apparent that the critical correlates were governmental characteristics; and they statistically explained 95 per cent of the interstate variation. The contrasting regressions indicate that the factors affecting a current level of spending differ markedly from those affecting the direction and magnitude of change in spending.

The findings about changes in expenditures, which were discussed in Chapter III, help to explain the present differences in the correlates of current and changing expenditures. Recall (Table III–7) that expenditures do not show consistent rates of growth from one time period to the next. Throughout the twentieth century, changes in expenditures have

TABLE IV–6

Coefficients of Simple Correlation
between Independent Variables and Each Measure of 1962–1965 Change
in Total State Government Expenditures per Capita

|  | *Percentage Change* | *Dollar Change* |
|---|---|---|
| SOCIO-ECONOMIC MEASURES |  |  |
| personal income (2)[a] | —.08 | —.19 |
| personal income per capita (3) | .21 | .24 |
| urbanization (4) | .19 | .12 |
| population (5) | —.13 | —.25 |
| population growth (6) | .14 | .21 |
| labor force in manufacturing (7) | —.36* | —.52* |
| value added by manufacturing per capita (8) | —.16 | —.29* |
| adults with college education (9) | .41* | .51* |
| families with low income (10) | —.29* | —.32* |
| population density (11) | —.07 | —.16 |
| area (12) | .15 | .21 |
| non-agricultural labor force (13) | —.03 | —.05 |
| non-white population (14) | —.19 | —.23 |
| population foreign-born or of foreign or mixed parentage (15) | .14 | .12 |
| POLITICAL MEASURES |  |  |
| voter turnout for U.S. Representative election (16) | .34* | .37* |
| voter turnout for gubernatorial election (17) | .33* | .36* |
| party competition in lower house (18)[b,c] | .17 | .17 |
| party competition in upper house (19)[b,c] | .19 | .23 |
| party competition in U.S. Representative election (20)[c] | .25 | .18 |
| party competition in gubernatorial election (21)[c] | .16 | .19 |
| gubernatorial tenure (22) | .35* | .36* |
| legislative compensation (23) | —.13 | —.20 |
| bills introduced per session (24) | .02 | —.06 |
| bills passed per session (25) | .07 | —.10 |
| length of legislative session (26) | —.06 | —.16 |
| financial support of legislature (27) | .11 | .23 |
| S-P index of malapportionment (28) | .03 | —.01 |
| D-K index of malapportionment (29) | —.17 | —.24 |
| D-E index of malapportionment (30) | —.11 | —.12 |
| lower-house tenure (31) | .25 | .19 |
| upper-house tenure (32) | .16 | .12 |
| number of legislators (33) | —.26 | —.35* |
| GOVERNMENTAL MEASURES |  |  |
| federal aid (34) | .10 | .28* |
| tax effort (35) | .00 | .22 |
| income tax per capita (36) | .31* | .35* |
| sales tax per capita (37) | —.03 | .01 |

TABLE IV–6 (Continued)

|  | Percentage Change | Dollar Change |
|---|---|---|
| GOVERNMENTAL MEASURES (Continued) |  |  |
| excise tax per capita (38) | .03 | .15 |
| income tax as % of total taxes (39) | .03 | .38* |
| sales tax as % of total taxes (40) | .25 | .44* |
| excise tax as % of total taxes (41) | .22 | .33* |
| state % of state-local expenditures (42) | .12 | .19 |
| % of state-local revenues to state (43) | —.05 | .16 |
| revenues from non-local sources (44) | —.07 | .28* |
| local expenditures per capita (45) | .05 | .18 |
| salaries of state employees (46) | .19 | .14 |
| employees per population (47) | .05 | .58* |
| 1962 total expenditures per capita | .33* | .61* |

*Significant at the .05 level.
[a]See note a in Table IV–1.
[b]See note b in Table IV–1.
[c]See note c in Table IV–1.

shown negative relationships with previous changes in expenditures. States' spending seems to increase in spurts, and a period of relative increase follows a period of stability or relative decline in expenditures. The fact that these spurts begin at different times in different states may clarify why a regression analysis of 48 states' changes in expenditures leaves unexplained much of the interstate variation for a specific period (e.g., 1962–1965). Immediate and transient phenomena, including the motivations and strengths of specific individuals and organizations, may exercise considerable influence on the increments of change which occur at any one time. But why is it possible for a set of governmental and economic characteristics to explain statistically almost all of the interstate variation in the level of current spending? Perhaps the levels reached by the annual growth of many years' budgeting reflect the continuing impact of governmental and economic characteristics. While the increment during any particular spending period may represent a relative rise or decline of a state's spending position in relation to the nation-wide trends, that increment generally is not so large as to change the *historical* position of that state's spending in relation to others. Both before and after the increment of change is recorded, there is a similar relationship between current spending and such factors as previous spending, taxes, federal aid, the state-local relationship, government employees, and the nature of economic conditions.

TABLE IV–7

Coefficients of Multiple Determination
Associated with the Most Powerful Independent Variables,
as Determined by Step-wise Regression

| Dependent Variable: 1962–1965 Percentage Change in Total Expenditures per Capita | |
|---|---|
| *Variables Added* | $R^2$ |
| Adults with college education | .17 |
| Labor force in manufacturing | .24 |
| Voter turnout for gubernatorial election | .30 |
| Legislative compensation | .34 |
| Bills passed per session | .40 |
| Gubernatorial tenure | .44 |
| Number of legislators | .47 |
| Legislative compensation | .50 |

| Dependent Variable: 1962–1965 Change in Dollars of Total Expenditures per Capita | |
|---|---|
| *Variables Added* | $R^2$ |
| 1962 total expenditures per capita | .37 |
| Adults with college education | .47 |
| Employees per population | .52 |
| Sales tax as % of total taxes | .57 |
| Income tax per capita | .64 |

## SUMMARY

This chapter has examined statistical relationships among current spending, measures of change in spending, and 46 measures of governmental, political, and socio-economic characteristics of the states. It began with the conclusion of Chapter III and sought to identify the factors that work along with the level of previous expenditures to influence state spending.

The principal findings are:

(1) Previous expenditures continue to show the strongest association with current spending when considered in controlled re-

lationships along with numerous other potential influences on spending.

(2) Measures of governmental and socio-economic characteristics, including federal aid, taxes, state-local financial relationships, state employees, population, urbanization, and industrialization, show significant relationships to current spending while controlling for the influence of previous spending.

(3) A step-wise regression analysis highlights three governmental characteristics (previous spending, the state percentage of state-local expenditures, and local government expenditures) as having the strongest independent relationships to the level of total current spending.

(4) Measures of economic activity (especially population, urbanization, and industrialization) show inverse relationships to state spending. This contrasts with the findings of other authors who examine the correlates of combined state and local government spending and seems to reflect the tendency of state governments in underdeveloped economies to assume more than the average portion of spending responsibilities.

(5) The variables considered in this book are more successful in accounting for interstate variation in current spending than in measures of spending change. This finding may reflect the fact that levels of expenditure represent the accretion of increments over long time spans in response to economic and governmental characteristics of a jurisdiction. In contrast, the particular increments of change occurring during a particular period may represent responses to more immediate and transient phenomena, including the motivations and resources of individual public officials, newspapers, or interest groups.

In the following chapter, this book turns away from the correlates of individual states' expenditures. Chapter V deals with historical experiences of the national economy and with international affairs that have affected changes in the level of states' spending throughout the country; but there will not be a complete break in the theme of analysis. After discussing general changes that have occurred in government spending during critical historical periods, Chapter V describes how these changes in spending are consistent with the findings of Chapter IV. In particular, it will describe how spending changes of the depression, of World War II, of the Korean Conflict, and of postwar periods occurred along with changes in taxes, in federal aids, in the state-local financial relationships, in government employees, and in the states' economies.

## CHAPTER V

# International Affairs,
# the National Economy,
# and Government Expenditures

### INTRODUCTION

THE PRINCIPAL TASK of this chapter is to assess the impact upon state government expenditures of major events in the recent history of international affairs and in the domestic economy. Since these events have also had a profound influence on the spending of the national and local governments, this chapter places the history of state government spending in the context of all American government spending throughout the twentieth century. It should help to demonstrate that state government expenditures do not operate in isolation from other components of American government. Just as the correlation coefficients of Chapter IV show that levels of state spending depend partly upon receipts from federal aids and upon the division of responsibilities between state and local authorities within each state, so the findings of this chapter will show that governments at all levels responded to common historical phenomena with dramatic changes in spending. Yet the responses to the common stimuli have not been identical: by charting the different tracks that federal, state, and local governments have taken during the depression, wars, and postwar reconversions, this chapter identifies salient differences in revenue systems, constitutional flexibility, and capacity for innovation that characterize each level of government in the United States.

In contrast to Chapters III and IV, this analysis does not deal with neat lists of dependent and independent variables that lend themselves to the crisp analysis of interstate spending variations. Instead, it considers the influence on state spending coming from the historical phenomena of the depression, World War II, the Korean Conflict, and two postwar reconversions. These episodes do not have opening and closing dates that have earned agreement from the universe of social scientists. While some observers date the beginning of the depression with the stock market crash of 1929, others point to severe levels of unemployment in certain agricultural areas and New England mill towns several years earlier when much of the country still viewed itself as prosperous. Roughly speaking, the depression ended with the employment boom of World War II; but this revitalization began before the actual opening of hostilities occurred in December, 1941. So an assessment of that war's impact on the spending of American state governments might profit from a definition of its beginning that includes some months of prewar mobilization.

There is a basic problem in sorting out the influence relationships considered here. The confusion is between international affairs *per se* and the domestic economic occurrences that are stimulated by international events. In the case of changes in state expenditures which coincided with the Second World War and the Korean Conflict, it appears that the response was to several domestic phenomena that were triggered by the wars. These factors include the war-related demands for economic and personnel resources which took precedence over civilian claims and the changes in the level of prosperity that were associated with war-stimulated industrial activity.

Another analytic problem arises from the possibility that the phenomena of depression, war and postwar reconversion changed the meaning of state expenditure data at the same time that they had an impact on the real level of spending. Population increases, changes in the magnitude of economic resources, and decreases in the purchasing power of the dollar have confounded the significance of the dollars spent by state governments. Before this analysis can proceed, it will be necessary to devise a standard of measurement that remains oblivious of these changes. If a standard measure is not employed, the findings that are reported may inflate or deflate the changes that actually occurred in the level of economic resources spent by state governments.[1]

[1]It was not necessary to correct the expenditure data used in Chapters III and IV for changes in the level of economic resources or the purchasing power of the dollar. In those chapters, the focus was not on changes in the level of expenditures, but on interstate variations in state spending at several points in time. Where the concern in those chapters was with changes in expenditures, the subject was changes in interstate variations (usually over short periods of time), rather than changes in spending levels *per se.*

## MEASUREMENTS

During this century a number of occurrences have influenced the meaning of government expenditures. This chapter focuses on changes in spending levels over time. It is therefore necessary at the outset to identify possible causes of confusion in the available information and to establish ground rules for dealing with the problems.

Inflation, increases in population, and increases in available economic resources can distort the meaning of state government expenditures. If this chapter fails to take account of changes in the population and the economy, it will overlook the obvious facts that expenditures in raw dollars increase partly to provide established services to a growing clientele, partly because inflation diminishes the productivity of each dollar that is spent, and partly because a growing economy has made it possible to increase expenditures without increasing the government's demands on available resources.

By correcting expenditures for population increases and for changes in the value of the dollar, it is possible to avoid a gross exaggeration of increases in spending. Between 1932 and 1962, uncorrected expenditures in current dollars for major domestic functions by federal, state, and local governments increased by 811 per cent: from $8.7 billion to $79.3 billion. This *appearance* of increase changes substantially after corrections are applied for population growth and inflation. Expenditures *per capita* in *constant dollars* (in 1954 dollars) increased by only 86 per cent over the 30-year period: from $177.18 to $329.28.

By calculating government expenditures as a percentage of Gross National Product, it is possible to ascertain changes in the demands that governments make on available resources. In these terms, spending by all governments for major domestic functions has been no greater in recent years than in the 1930's: 14.9 per cent of GNP in 1932 and 14.3 per cent of GNP in 1962.

One of the topics considered below is the change in state government spending relative to that of other governments in the United States. Yet if this chapter fails to take into account changes in the responsibilities of the federal government, it will inflate the image of federal "encroachment" upon the activities of state and local governments.[2] In order to keep year-by-year comparisons of federal, state, and local expenditures on a basis that permits the identification of changes in the expenditures of each level of government for comparable purposes, the data include only those expenditures made for the functions pursued in common by all governments. It excludes expenditures for the peculiarly federal responsibilities of international affairs, defense, space exploration,

[2]Frederick C. Mosher and Orville F. Poland, *The Costs of American Governments: Facts, Trends, Myths* (New York: Dodd, Mead & Co., 1964), pp. 9–14.

postal service, and interest on the national debt.[3] Federal expenditures for these functions have increased dramatically from 39 per cent of the federal budget in 1940 to 73 per cent in 1962. To compare changes in *all* federal expenditures to changes in state and local government expenditures would develop an unreal image of a devouring federal behemoth.

In the analyses that follow, the measures of spending vary with the issues at hand. When the concern is spending by all governments (federal, state, and local) for common functions, the measure is expenditures per capita in constant dollars or expenditures as a percentage of Gross National Product. When the concern is the distribution of spending between levels of government, the measure is the percentage of spending for common functions by federal, state, and local governments. When the concern is the distribution of spending between the major public services, the measure is the percentage of spending made by all governments for education, highways, public welfare, health and hospitals, natural resources, public safety, and general government.[4]

In order to have consistent data from one analysis to the next, the expenditure information included in Tables V–1, V–2, V–3 and V–4 comes from a single source: *Historical Statistics on Governmental Finances and Employment,* a volume of the *Census of Governments 1962.* The analysis suffers from some limitations of the data: there are constant dollar expenditure figures only for the 1932–1962 period, and prior to 1952, there are data only for selected years.[5] Given the limitations of the data source, the following points mark the beginning and end of major events: (1) the depression is from 1932 to 1940; (2) World War II (including the prewar mobilization) is from 1940 to 1944; (3) the post-World War II period is from 1946 to 1950; and (4) the Korean Conflict is from 1950 to 1953.

## CHANGES IN GOVERNMENT SPENDING FOR COMMON DOMESTIC FUNCTIONS

Between 1932 and 1962, total common-function expenditures (per capita constant dollars) by federal, state, and local governments in-

[3]The interest on the national debt is considered peculiarly federal because the bulk of it results from wartime expenditures. See R. A. Musgrave and J. M. Culbertson, "The Growth of Public Expenditures in the United States, 1890–1948," *National Tax Journal,* 6 (June 1953): 97–115.

[4]Where the focus is on changes in the distribution of expenditures between levels of government (combining *all* states or localities) or between services, it is not necessary to control for changes in population, purchasing power, or economic resources. During any given year when percentage distributions are calculated, these potentially disturbing factors are assumed to be constant for each level of government or each field of service.

[5]The years included in the volume are: 1902, 1913, 1922, 1927, 1932, and every second year to 1952, and then every year to 1962.

creased with the depression, decreased during World War II and the Korean Conflict, and increased in postwar years. Table V–1 shows changes in expenditures by year.

The increases of the depression were most dramatic from 1934 to 1936. As Table V–2 suggests, these changes reflect additions to programs in the fields of natural resources and public welfare.[6] New fed-

TABLE V–1

All Governments' Expenditures per Capita (in 1954 Dollars)
for Common Functions

| Years | Per Capita Expenditures | |
|---|---|---|
| 1962 | $329.28 | |
| 1961 | 313.71 | |
| 1960 | 292.53 | |
| 1959 | 293.98 | |
| 1958 | 276.96 | |
| 1957 | 267.58 | |
| 1956 | 263.64 | |
| 1955 | 256.48 | |
| 1954 | 251.40 | |
| 1953 | 235.21 | |
| 1952 | 220.21 | War |
| 1950 | 250.55 | |
| 1948 | 205.28 | Reconversion |
| 1946 | 176.73 | |
| 1944 | 211.47 | |
| 1942 | 180.96 | War |
| 1940 | 239.91 | |
| 1938 | 225.21 | |
| 1936 | 233.52 | Depression |
| 1934 | 177.65 | |
| 1932 | 177.18 | |

[6]Kendrick suggests that these programs, initiated during the depression, might have come without the economic crisis. He sees them following upon changes in public attitudes toward government services; and these attitudes began to appear *prior* to the depression. He speculates that the trend of the 1930's brought to a head the developments that were moving in the direction of New Deal types of programs. See Myron Slade Kendrick, *A Century and a Half of Federal Expenditures* (New York: National Bureau of Economic Research, 1955), pp. 33–35.

**TABLE V-2**

Percentage of Total Spending Allocated for Each Major Field[a]

| | 1962 | 1953 | 1950 | 1944 | 1940 | 1932 | 1922 | 1913 | 1902 |
|---|---|---|---|---|---|---|---|---|---|
| Education | 28.8% | 27.4% | 29.3% | 15.1% | 19.7% | 26.6% | 28.5% | 25.3% | 23.1% |
| Highways | 13.3 | 13.7 | 11.8 | 6.5 | 15.2 | 20.2 | 21.6 | 18.2 | 15.7 |
| Public welfare | 6.5 | 8.0 | 9.0 | 6.2 | 9.2 | 5.1 | 2.1 | 2.5 | 3.7 |
| Health and hospitals | 10.1 | 11.4 | 10.3 | 5.8 | 6.3 | 9.2 | 10.5 | 9.1 | 10.2 |
| Natural resources | 16.4 | 13.8 | 16.1 | 15.4 | 19.5 | 5.4 | 3.7 | 4.4 | 22.5 |
| Public safety | 4.2 | 4.6 | 3.8 | 4.0 | 4.3 | 6.4 | 4.5 | 7.3 | 8.1 |
| General government | 2.8 | 5.1 | 4.7 | 5.9 | 5.1 | 6.9 | 7.3 | 11.1 | 15.7 |

[a] "Total spending" here means "all governments' expenditures for common functions."

eral programs provided the major stimuli of these increases. Programs that were begun or enlarged in those years included surplus-commodity distribution, wildlife restoration, soil conservation, support for grazing lands, price parity, old-age assistance, aid to families with dependent children, aid to the blind, and child welfare.

In both the Second World War and the Korean Conflict, there was a sharp, initial drop in domestic spending, which was followed by moderate increases. Much of the decrease in spending reflects the scarcity of resources which was caused by the wars. Manpower, capital, equipment, and materials became less available for civilian purposes and precluded many opportunities for state, local, and federal agencies to spend at previous levels.[7] Only one domestic field showed relative increases in expenditures during both wars: spending for *general government* increased from 5.1 to 5.9 per cent of the total during the 1940–1944 period; and it increased from 4.7 to 5.1 per cent of the total during the 1950–1953 period. These increases appeared at state and local as well as at federal levels. They may reflect the increase in economic regulatory activities that came along with war mobilization. Wartime lessening of spending for public welfare and education reflected, in part, reductions in the number of clients for these services. The decline in welfare payments was the result of wartime increases in prosperity.[8] The reductions in educational expenditures may represent wartime drains on college enrollments or the feeling that an investment in culture must wait until hostilities end.

Education and highways benefited most from increased spending in the postwar years; both fields almost doubled their share of spending between 1944 and 1950. Education again increased its share of spending after the Korean Conflict, while highway expenditures held constant at that time. Even a constant share of aggregate spending was desirable in the 1953–1962 period when per capita expenditures for common functions increased from $235.28 to $329.28 (in 1954 dollars). The dramatic increases in spending which followed the wars reflect not only the need to make repairs and capital improvements that were postponed during the wars, but also the need to serve the returning veterans and, later, their children. Population increases required vast capital expenditures for new primary schools during the late 1940's. By the 1960's, the generation of war babies had advanced through the grades to college and graduate school; and they also required public hospitals, correctional institutions, recreational facilities, and highways. At each stage of their lives, war

[7]Mosher and Poland, *Costs of American Governments*, pp. 24–29.
[8]See Gilbert Y. Steiner, *Social Insecurity: The Politics of Welfare* (Chicago: Rand McNally & Co., 1966), pp. 30–31.

babies (and now their children) have stimulated increases in local, state, and federal budgets.[9]

Events in international relations and the national economy have not only affected the level of spending per capita in constant dollars; they have also influenced governments' demands on available financial resources. Table V–3 shows changes in expenditures as a percentage of GNP from 1902 through 1962. Incidents of dramatic spending change

TABLE V–3
All Governments' Common-Function Expenditures as Percentages of
Gross National Product

| Years | % of GNP |
|:-----:|:--------:|
| 1962 | 14.3% |
| 1961 | 14.2 |
| 1960 | 13.1 |
| 1959 | 13.1 |
| 1958 | 12.7 |
| 1957 | 11.8 |
| 1956 | 11.5 |
| 1955 | 11.0 |
| 1954 | 11.2 |
| 1953 | 10.1 |
| 1952 | 9.7 War |
| 1950 | 11.6 |
| 1948 | 9.5 Reconversion |
| 1946 | 8.2 |
| 1944 | 8.8 |
| 1942 | 9.1 War |
| 1940 | 14.2 |
| 1938 | 15.3 |
| 1936 | 15.9 Depression |
| 1934 | 14.8 |
| 1932 | 14.9 |
| 1927 | 8.2 |
| 1922 | 8.1 |
| 1913 | 5.7 |
| 1902 | 4.6 |

[9]Mosher and Poland, *Costs of American Governments*, p. 30.

occurred between 1927 and 1932 at the onset of the depression and in the early war years of 1940–1942 and 1950–1952. The 1927–1932 *increase* reflects, principally, the economic depression. Governments' use of available resources increased markedly as GNP dropped from $96.3 billion to $58.5 billion, while expenditures increased only slightly from $7.9 billion to $8.7 billion. The wartime *decreases* in domestic expenditures as a percentage of GNP reflect a great increase in the economy and a de-emphasis of domestic spending. Gross National Product increased 59 per cent from 1940 to 1942 and 22 per cent from 1950 to 1952. During the same periods, government expenditures for common domestic functions increased only 1.4 and 0.3 per cent. In the period from the Korean War to 1962, common-function expenditures moved slowly upward as a percentage of GNP, along with increases in both the national economy and government spending: from 1953 to 1962, GNP increased 52 per cent, and common-function spending increased 115 per cent. *As late as 1962, however, governments were not spending as much of the available resources for common domestic functions as they were in the 1930's.*

The depression, the wars, and the postwar periods have also left their mark on the division of responsibilities between federal, state, and local governments. Table V–4 shows the percentage of total spending for common domestic functions by level of government in selected years between 1902 and 1962.[10] Federal and state governments have acquired a larger share of financial responsibilities, while the local governments have lost some of their share over the 60-year period. The federal share increased most dramatically during the depression and World War II. Between 1932 and 1944, the federal government increased its spending for common functions from 14 to 58 per cent of the total. The federal increase during the depression reflects, in part, the federal government's relative isolation from economic catastrophe. Unlike state and local governments, the federal government did not suffer from the diminution of the real property tax base; and compared to most state and local officials, federal officials may have been philosophically better prepared to fight the depression with new programs and increased spending. Wartime increases in the federal share reflect the greater access of federal agencies to scarce manpower and material, as well as the federal development of

[10]The totals in Table V–4 add to more than 100 per cent because the spending for each level of government includes both direct and intergovernmental spending in each government's share of expenditures. This calculation recognizes the influence that accrues to a spending agency from money granted to other levels of government and from money received from other levels of government. As grantor, an agency may influence the final use of its funds. As recipient, an agency often has wide discretion in the application of intergovernmental funds.

**TABLE V–4**

Percentage of Total Spending by Federal, State, and Local Governments[a]

| | 1962 | 1953 | 1950 | 1944 | 1940 | 1932 | 1922 | 1913 | 1902 |
|---|---|---|---|---|---|---|---|---|---|
| Federal | 33.8% | 32.1% | 38.0% | 58.0% | 41.8% | 13.6% | 15.2% | 10.9% | 9.9% |
| State | 39.4 | 39.8 | 37.3 | 24.3 | 30.6 | 31.7 | 22.3 | 16.9 | 16.7 |
| Local | 50.2[b] | 50.5 | 44.9 | 33.4 | 45.4 | 66.5 | 69.6 | 76.8 | 78.7 |

[a]"Total spending" here means "all governments' expenditures for common functions."
[b]Percentages sum to more than 100 because intergovernmental expenditures are counted twice: once for the granting level and once for the level of final expenditure. See note 10 of this chapter.

domestic programs to help the war effort. One war-related domestic expenditure provided ports and canals: between 1940 and 1944, federal expenditures for water-transport facilities increased from $321 million to $4.5 billion. Between 1944 and 1962, the federal share of common-function expenditures declined from 58 to 34 per cent, and both state and local governments increased their shares of total spending.

The states have shown almost consistent growth in their share of expenditures since 1902, while the local governments' share of spending has fluctuated widely. The states' share of domestic spending increased from 17 to 32 per cent up until 1932, while the local governments' share was declining from 79 to 67 per cent. In the 1930's, the states' share remained stable, while the local governments' share declined further to 45 per cent of the total. During World War II, the states lost some ground, but the local governments continued to lose ground at an even faster pace.

The greater stability of state government spending during the trauma of depression reflects the more flexible resource position of state governments. The depression was severe in its attack on the tax base of local governments—the value of real property. Local governments face the prohibitions of state constitutions when they consider expanding their revenue systems, and many local authorities did not have sufficient sources of wealth to support the service needs of their communities.[11] Even in poor states, however, state governments have access to pockets of resources which their general revenue systems can tap and redistribute to needy sections. Furthermore, state governments have more discretion than local governments in shifting the nature of their tax base. At the beginning of the depression, state governments depended heavily upon the property tax; but, beginning with Mississippi, 23 states adopted a general sales tax during the 1930's.[12] This tax is less susceptible to economic adversity than is the property tax. The reason for this may be that retail sales fall off less sharply during severe depression than do property values.[13] Finally, the states received more benefits from major new federal programs than did the cities. Between 1932 and 1940, states began to receive assistance for agricultural conservation, child health services,

[11]Dick Netzer, *Economics of the Property Tax* (Washington: Brookings Institution, 1965), pp. 6, 186.

[12]John F. Due, *State Sales Tax Administration* (Chicago: Public Administration Service, 1963), p. 3. Between 1932 and 1940, the percentage of state tax revenue received from property taxes dropped from 17 per cent to 8 per cent.

[13]During 1962, the coefficients of simple correlation between per capita personal income and per capita state and local government receipts from each of the following taxes testifies to the economic dependence of the property tax: property tax, .55; personal income tax, .25; general sales tax, .01; and excise taxes, .35.

aid to dependent children, and old-age payments. State receipts of federal aid increased by $445 million, while municipal receipts increased by only $268 million during the 1932–1940 period.

One of the findings reported in Chapter III also testifies to the capacity of resource-poor state governments to meet the demands of the depression in a positive fashion. Coefficients of variability for twelve separate years between 1903 and 1965 show that in the period including the depression (1929–1939), there was the greatest *narrowing of the dispersion* of low- and high-spending states around the national average. (See Table III–4.) Taking these findings in conjunction with those showing increases in state spending during the depression, it is evident that low-spending states narrowed the gap between themselves and the high-spending states, despite the depression's threat to their resource base.

Although the analyses of Chapters IV and V have employed markedly different techniques, their findings can complement one another in helping to explain why some state governments have come to spend more than others. Chapter IV found significant positive levels of association between measures of state spending and federal aid, state taxes, the share of state and local finances assumed by the state, and the size of the state bureaucracy; and it found negative relationships between spending and population, urbanization, and industrialization. This chapter has employed a simple comparison of time series in expenditures that correspond with major historical episodes. Despite the simplicity of the statistics, it has found certain sharp changes in spending which occur along with depression, wars, and postwar reconversions. The question to be faced now is: Do the findings of Chapter IV help to explain the changes in state spending which are observed in Chapter V?[14]

A joint examination of findings from Chapters IV and V leads to the inference that the events of depression, war, and postwar reconversion influenced state expenditures by first having an impact on the economic resources and several governmental characteristics of the states.

During the depression, it appears that economic events worked to increase state spending through a decline in the economic resources within each state. Complementing this factor were changes in state taxes and federal aids, and changes in the financial relationship between state and local governments. Despite depression-related cuts in receipts from established taxes, state revenues benefited from new taxes on retail sales and also from federal aids for agriculture, for child health, for dependent

[14]The following speculation is based on the assumption that correlates of 1962 spending generally reflect relationships between similar characteristics and spending during earlier years.

children, and for the aged. Perhaps because of the state governments' more favorable resource position, the balance of state-local financial responsibilities tipped toward state governments: the state share of state and local expenditures increased from 36 to 48 per cent during the 1932–1940 period. With these changes in governmental characteristics, the states' spending increased by 84 per cent during the 1932–1940 period, while local spending increased by only 21 per cent.[15]

The relatively stagnant spending of World War II and the Korean Conflict corresponded with marked increases in state economic resources, but also with stagnation in other critical characteristics of state governments. States' receipts from federal aid declined markedly during the wars. Between 1940 and 1942 and between 1950 and 1952, receipts from federal aid increased only $77 million and $54 million respectively; they had increased by $450 million and $1,473 million during the earlier peacetime years of 1932–1940 and 1946–1950 respectively. The wars also affected manpower availability and the size of state bureaucracies. The number of nonfederal government employees *declined* by 174,000 between 1940 and 1944.[16] The number of state employees increased by only 25,000 during the 1950–1953 period, although it increased by 148,000 and 211,000 in the three-year periods before and after the Korean war.

The availability of manpower for domestic purposes supported spending increases during the postwar reconversion. From 1946 to 1962, state employees per 10,000 population increased by 109 per cent. Also, during the postwar years, the need to make up for postponed capital expenditures and to provide for population increases appeared to stimulate increases in tax effort and federal aids. State taxes increased from 2.8 to 4.7 per cent of personal income from 1946 to 1962, and federal grants increased from 13 to 23 per cent of state revenue. Significant new federal programs in the postwar period included aids for federally impacted school districts, national defense education, and interstate highways.

While events in international affairs and in the national economy seem to have worked their influence on state expenditures through the intermediaries of state economies and governmental characteristics, the phenomena of incremental budgeting and previous expenditures helped to isolate the spending of each state from its environment. Throughout the periods of increase and decline that affected states generally, the influences on individual states were not so great that public officials ig-

---

[15]These figures do not compensate for changes in population, economic resources, or purchasing power.

[16]Data about state government employees are not available for the years 1940 and 1944.

nored the constraints imposed by earlier budgets. Budgeteers continued to rely on previous expenditures as a major criterion in their financial planning. Changes occurred incrementally from the bases of established spending; there were few cases of changes great enough to alter the relative positions of states. The data of Table III–1 testify to the conservative bias of incremental budgeting. Although state spending has shown great increases throughout this century—even while controlling for changes in population, for inflation, and for the magnitude of available resources—there remains a great resemblance between the interstate differentials in spending today and those of several generations past.

## SUMMARY

This chapter has examined the record of state spending in the context of the spending of all American governments for common domestic functions. It has also examined the influences upon all states' spending during major historical episodes and has compared these findings with the influences on individual states' spending by the economic and governmental variables that were considered in Chapter IV.

Expressed in constant dollars per capita, all governments' spending for common domestic functions increased during the depression, declined during wartime, and increased again in postwar years. Expressed as percentages of Gross National Product, all governments' common-function spending reached its height during the low GNP years of the depression. It was then that American governments spent the largest portion of available economic resources. During the war years of low domestic spending and high economic productivity, expenditures dropped as a percentage of GNP. After the wars, domestic spending increased gradually in relation to economic resources.

Relative to the spending of federal and local governments, *state spending* increased from 1902 to the depression, remained stable during the depression, fell during World War II, and increased after the war. In 1962, state spending accounted for 39 per cent of all governments' common-function expenditures. The states are in second place behind local governments and ahead of the federal government in expenditures for common functions.

During the 1930's, the states showed themselves to be more adaptable than local governments in the face of economic adversity. Partly because of more flexible constitutional provisions, a number of states made basic alterations in their revenue systems during the depression, and most states assumed a larger share of state-local spending responsibilities. State spending per capita (in constant dollars) increased by 35 per cent during the 1932–1940 period, while the per capita spending of local governments (in constant dollars) increased by only 3 per cent. During the same years, the state share of all governments' common-function spending declined by only 1 per cent, while the local governments' share declined by 21 per cent. Moreover, the low-spending states accommodated themselves to the depression in a fashion that caused the dispersion of high- and low-spending states to narrow markedly.

It appears that the events of depression, war, and postwar periods operate directly upon state economic and governmental characteristics and indirectly upon state spending. International affairs and the national economy work their influence through the components of economic resources, federal aid, state taxes, employees, or the state share of state-local finances. Because of incremental budget techniques, however, the level of each state's previous expenditures has helped to isolate its spending from major historical events. While the depression, war, and postwar reconversions have had their impact on state budget-makers, the impact has not been so profound as to upset basic patterns of interstate spending differentials. As noted in Chapter III, the differentials among states' spending that existed in 1903 are still recognizable in the spending of 1965.

# CHAPTER VI

# The Regional Affiliation of States
# and Government Spending*

THIS CHAPTER CONSIDERS the regional affiliations that influence state government expenditures. It begins with the assumption that there are differences in the politics, economics, and expenditure norms of states that are located in different sections of the country and proceeds to examine the impact that these differences have on state government expenditures.

The books and articles of V. O. Key, Frank Munger, Duane Lockard, Frank Jonas, Thomas Donnelly, and John Fenton have described at length the practices of political parties and electoral processes as they operate in the states of the South, the Middle West, the border states, New England, the Rocky Mountain area, and the Greater West.[1] Daniel Elazar has considered regional patterns in political culture and traces these patterns to the "geology" created by initial settlements and transcontinental migrations from these settlements.[2] The data of the Uni-

*This chapter has been adapted from the author's article "Regional Patterns in the Expenditures of American States" in the December 1967 issue of *Western Political Quarterly*.

[1]V. O. Key, *Southern Politics in State and Nation* (New York: Alfred A. Knopf, 1949); Duane Lockard, *New England State Politics* (Princeton, N.J.: Princeton University Press, 1959); John H. Fenton, *Midwest Politics* (New York: Holt, Rinehart & Winston, 1966); John H. Fenton, *Politics in the Border States* (New Orleans: Hauser Press, 1957); Frank Munger, ed., *American State Politics: Reading for Comparative Analysis* (New York: Thomas Y. Crowell Co., 1966); Frank H. Jonas, *Western Politics* (Salt Lake City: University of Utah Press, 1961); and Thomas R. Donnelly, *Rocky Mountain Politics* (Albuquerque: University of New Mexico Press, 1940).
[2]Daniel J. Elazar, *American Federalism: A View from the States* (New York: Thomas Y. Crowell Co., 1966).

versity of Michigan Survey Research Center document regional differences in attitudes toward public affairs.[3] The work of Harvey S. Perloff testifies to regional economic patterns that produce differences in personal well-being and in the character of industry and agriculture.[4] Unfortunately for the present analysis, none of these publications deals explicitly with regional variations in government expenditures or other aspects of public policy. Most of the work by political scientists has focused on party-electoral aspects of politics in a single region. While the Elazar and Perloff volumes have considered a variety of regions across the United States, they have not dealt systematically with the policies of state and local governments. As a result, one is left only with the impression that differences in economics, politics, and historical experiences that are common to neighboring states might leave their impact on state government expenditures.

The theory and findings of Chapters I to V give no clear indication about the impact of the states' regional affiliations on their spending. Generally, there are weak relationships between political characteristics and expenditures; but it is possible that certain regions have concentrations of political phenomena which are strong enough to influence the level of state spending. Southern states show marked deviations from the 48-state averages in the direction of little party competition, poorly apportioned legislatures, low voter turnout, and stringent suffrage regulations. Moreover, survey research generally finds southern respondents to be conservative in their attitudes toward social welfare programs, as well as toward civil rights. The political culture of the South might be sufficiently conservative to work against state government expenditures. Yet the underdeveloped economy of the South—if the findings of Chapter IV apply—should work in favor of high state expenditures.

The contemporary practices of state officials, as well as the residue of history and economics, may have an impact on regional differences in spending. There is some evidence that state administrators and legislators consciously adjust their programs and levels of spending to their perceptions of regional norms. State officials feel that neighboring states have problems and resources that resemble their own. Many officials also believe that they are competing with other states in their region for new

[3] See V. O. Key, *Public Opinion and American Democracy* (New York: Alfred A. Knopf, 1961), especially chapt. 5; and Angus Campbell *et al.*, *The American Voter* (New York: John Wiley & Sons, 1960), especially chapt. 16.

[4] Harvey S. Perloff *et al.*, *Regions, Resources, and Economic Growth* (Baltimore: Johns Hopkins University Press, 1960), and Lawrence A. Leonard, "State and Local Governmental Revenue Structures—A National and Regional Analysis," *National Tax Journal*, 11 (March 1958): 67–77.

industries. Both of these beliefs work in the direction of similar levels of taxation and spending among neighboring states.

As part of a survey among budget officers of 67 major agencies in the southern states of Florida, Georgia, Kentucky, and Mississippi,[5] an attempt was made to identify the states that served as the budgeteers' reference group. In this survey, the following question was asked:

> *Have you or any of your colleagues contacted officials in other states in an attempt to learn how they deal with a particular situation that you have encountered in your work?*

When a budget officer answered in the affirmative, he was then asked:

> *What states do you feel are the best sources of information?*

The 67 respondents made 198 nominations of states that were among the "best sources of information." Eighty-seven per cent of their nominations were in the region that includes the 11 states of the Confederacy and the border states of Delaware, Maryland, Kentucky, West Virginia, and Oklahoma. Thirty-five per cent of the nominations were states that bordered directly on the states of the respondents. It is conceivable that southern officials are more parochial in their references than are officials in other regions. Nevertheless, these nominations suggest that the regional identifications of administrators may help to create similarities in the expenditures of neighboring states.

One of the tests performed in this chapter measures the presence of regional norms in state spending levels. In other tests, this chapter considers the following questions: What regional peculiarities exist in the expenditures of American states? To what extent do regional peculiarities in spending reflect regional peculiarities in state expenditure processes?

It is possible that states show regional patterns in expenditures while the essential processes of state expenditures prevail throughout the nation. Thus, the variables in Chapters III and IV which were found to be important correlates of spending for 48 states may operate similarly within each region. Even though the values of these characteristics (*i.e.*, state scores on previous expenditures, the state share of state-local finances, *et al.*) might vary from one region to another, the relationships among them may occur consistently from one region to the next. The states of one region might score consistently low on measures of previous expenditures, on the proportion of state-local responsibilities assumed by state agencies, on the size of the state bureaucracy, on federal aid, and

[5]A "major agency" was defined as one having a budget of at least $1 million during the year (1966) of the survey.

on state taxes. If these states also score low on current expenditures, they would present an instance of regional peculiarities in spending and other governmental characteristics, but not in the relationships among factors that exert their influence on spending.

## DEFINITIONS AND TECHNIQUES

It is no simple task to define regions within the United States. In each part of the country there are "border states" that might fit into any of several regions. Delaware, for example, might be in the South, border states, Northeast, or Mid-Atlantic; Illinois may be in the Northeast, North Central, Great Lakes, Middle West, or Plains. In order to minimize border disputes, this chapter employs three different demarcations of American regions. The first two are used by Perloff *et al.* in their study of regional economic development.[6] The first demarcation divides the 48 states into three regions. The Ohio and Mississippi Rivers are the principal boundaries of the *North, Southeast,* and *Transmississippi*.[7] Due to economic affinities, the states of Arkansas and Louisiana are included in the Southeast. In order to obtain greater precision, the second demarcation divides two of the regions of Demarcation 1. It separates North into *New England, Mid-Atlantic,* and *Great Lakes;* and it divides Transmississippi into *Plains, Mountains, Southwest,* and *Far West.* The third demarcation divides the 48 states into the four principal regions used in the reports of the United States Census Bureau. *Northeast* encompasses New England and the urban-industrial states of New York, New Jersey, and Pennsylvania; *North Central* includes the Great Lakes and Plains states; *South* includes the 11 states of the Confederacy plus the border states of Delaware, Maryland, West Virginia, Kentucky, and Oklahoma; and *Transplains* includes the remaining states of the mountain, desert, and Pacific coastal areas. The states in Demarcations 1, 2, and 3 are listed in Table VI–1.

This chapter employs the measures of state government expenditures in total and by major field of service which are used in Chapters III and IV. A comparison of regional means and coefficients of variability indicates regional differences in expenditures and the relative distinctiveness of each region's expenditures during the years from 1903 to 1965.[8]

---

[6]See Perloff *et al., Regions, Resources, and Economic Growth.*

[7]While the component states of Perloff's regional demarcations remain unchanged, his "West" is called "Transmississippi" here in order to avoid confusion with other designations. For a similar reason, the region that the Census Bureau names "West" is called "Transplains" here.

[8]Recall that coefficients of variability equal the standard deviation of a measure divided by its mean.

TABLE VI–1

Regional Demarcations of the American States

| *Demarcation 1* | *Demarcation 2* | *Demarcation 3* |
|---|---|---|
| NORTH | NEW ENGLAND | NORTHEAST |
| Maine | Maine | Maine |
| New Hampshire | New Hampshire | New Hampshire |
| Vermont | Vermont | Vermont |
| Massachusetts | Massachusetts | Massachusetts |
| Rhode Island | Rhode Island | Rhode Island |
| Connecticut | Connecticut | Connecticut |
| New York | | New York |
| New Jersey | MID-ATLANTIC | New Jersey |
| Pennsylvania | New York | Pennsylvania |
| Maryland | New Jersey | |
| Delaware | Pennsylvania | SOUTH |
| Ohio | Maryland | Delaware |
| Indiana | Delaware | Maryland |
| Illinois | | Virginia |
| Michigan | SOUTHEAST | West Virginia |
| Wisconsin | Virginia | North Carolina |
| | West Virginia | South Carolina |
| SOUTHEAST | North Carolina | Georgia |
| Virginia | South Carolina | Florida |
| West Virginia | Georgia | Kentucky |
| North Carolina | Florida | Tennessee |
| South Carolina | Kentucky | Alabama |
| Georgia | Tennessee | Mississippi |
| Florida | Alabama | Arkansas |
| Kentucky | Mississippi | Louisiana |
| Tennessee | Arkansas | Oklahoma |
| Alabama | Louisiana | Texas |
| Mississippi | | |
| Arkansas | GREAT LAKES | NORTH CENTRAL |
| Louisiana | Ohio | Ohio |
| | Indiana | Indiana |
| TRANSMISSISSIPPI | Illinois | Illinois |
| Minnesota | Michigan | Michigan |
| Iowa | Wisconsin | Wisconsin |
| Missouri | | Minnesota |
| North Dakota | PLAINS | Iowa |
| South Dakota | Minnesota | Missouri |
| Nebraska | Iowa | North Dakota |
| Kansas | Missouri | South Dakota |
| Oklahoma | North Dakota | Kansas |
| Texas | South Dakota | Nebraska |
| Montana | Nebraska | |
| Wyoming | Kansas | TRANSPLAINS |
| Colorado | | Montana |
| | MOUNTAINS | Wyoming |
| | Montana | |

97

TABLE VI–1 (Continued)

| Demarcation 1 | Demarcation 2 | Demarcation 3 |
|---|---|---|
| TRANSMISSISSIPPI (Cont.) | MOUNTAINS (Cont.) | TRANSPLAINS (Cont.) |
| New Mexico | Wyoming | Colorado |
| Idaho | Colorado | New Mexico |
| Utah | Idaho | Idaho |
| Arizona | Utah | Utah |
| Oregon | | Arizona |
| Washington | SOUTHWEST | Washington |
| Nevada | Oklahoma | Oregon |
| California | Texas | Nevada |
| | New Mexico | California |
| | Arizona | |
| | FAR WEST | |
| | Washington | |
| | Oregon | |
| | Nevada | |
| | California | |

By comparing coefficients of variability for each region to the coefficients for the nation as a whole, it will be possible to assess the relative distinctiveness of regional as opposed to national spending patterns. These data will support inferences concerning the relative importance of regional and national norms to state government expenditures.

In order to assess the regional impact on the discrete spending influences identified in Chapters III and IV, this chapter compares regional expenditures in 1962 to those predicted for each region by a nationwide model of the expenditure system. Where regional expenditures actually resemble those predicted, it is concluded that regional expenditures respond to the factors that influence state spending generally. Where this happens, it is evident that regional peculiarities in expenditures reflect consistent regional peculiarities in governmental characteristics. A multiple regression equation, produced by the step-wise technique of Chapter IV, provides the nationwide model of the state expenditure system. The equation shows numerical relationships among independent variables and constants which produce the values of a dependent variable (expenditures). The equation takes the form:

$$Y = a + b_1X_1 + b_2X_2 + b_3X_3$$

$X$ represents the values of the independent variables that are identified as showing the strongest independent relationships to total current spending per capita. These variables are: previous spending, the state share of state-local finances, and local government expenditures per capita. The *a* and *b* are constants that, when multiplied and added to the values of the independent variables, result in a value (*Y*) that approximates the magnitude of expenditures.

By means of this regression equation, it is possible to assess whether expenditures of states in a specific region respond to the same system that influences state expenditures generally. When the values of the average characteristics of states in a region are substituted for the values of the independent variables, the equation serves to estimate the average state expenditures in the region. The ratio between the actual value and the estimated value of the expenditures indicates the correspondence between the items relating to state expenditures in a particular region and the items relating to state expenditures throughout the United States. For regions where this ratio is far removed from 1.00 (obtained where the expenditures estimated on the basis of a 48-state regression model equal the real expenditures of states in the region), it is apparent that factors affecting state expenditures in the region are not identical with those affecting state expenditures throughout the nation. In other words, the application of the 48-state regression model to each region can identify those regions in which the "typical" set of variables fails to relate with state expenditures in the "typical" manner.

## REGIONAL DIFFERENCES IN EXPENDITURES

There are clear regional differences in the expenditures of American states. This is made evident by the data of Table VI–2, which expresses the average expenditures of states in each region as a percentage of the average state expenditures over the nation as a whole.

States in northern and eastern regions (including states north of the Ohio River and as far west as the Plains) tend to score low on expenditures per capita for education, public welfare, and natural resources, but high on expenditures for health and hospitals, public safety, and general government. The low state expenditures for education may reflect the regional emphasis on local financing for that service, plus the relatively high reliance on private schools (especially Roman Catholic parochial schools). Low spending for natural resources may be a product of high population congestion in most of these regions and also the result of relatively little governmental attention given to resource development. High expenditures for public safety, especially in the New England and Mid-Atlantic states, reflect well-developed state police forces in those areas.

Western regions (Transplains, Mountain, Far West, Transmississippi, and Southwest) score high on most expenditures, especially in the fields of education, highways, and natural resources. The large high-

TABLE VI-2

Mean Expenditures per Capita of States in Each Region as Percentages of National Means, by Major Field, 1962

| | Total | Education | Highways | Public Welfare | Health and Hospitals | Natural Resources | Public Safety | General Government |
|---|---|---|---|---|---|---|---|---|
| North | .93 | .82 | .92 | .88 | 1.25 | .74 | 1.11 | 1.07 |
| New England | .99 | .65 | 1.12 | 1.05 | 1.40 | .99 | 1.24 | 1.31 |
| Mid-Atlantic | .95 | .99 | .75 | .73 | 1.40 | .58 | 1.15 | 2.86 |
| Great Lakes | .85 | .84 | .87 | .81 | .91 | .59 | .93 | .73 |
| Northeast | .93 | .69 | .95 | .95 | 1.35 | .85 | 1.13 | 1.23 |
| North Central | .89 | .83 | .98 | .88 | .94 | .84 | .88 | .73 |
| Plains | .92 | .82 | 1.07 | .92 | .95 | 1.01 | .85 | .75 |
| Transmississippi | 1.10 | 1.16 | 1.16 | 1.09 | .87 | 1.31 | 1.08 | 1.09 |
| Mountains | 1.18 | 1.24 | 1.47 | 1.00 | .84 | 1.76 | 1.07 | 1.25 |
| Far West | 1.33 | 1.46 | 1.15 | 1.23 | 1.00 | 1.71 | 1.71 | 1.59 |
| Transplains | 1.24 | 1.40 | 1.27 | 1.09 | .85 | 1.63 | 1.30 | 1.40 |
| Southwest | 1.08 | 1.33 | .93 | 1.34 | .64 | .87 | .84 | 1.03 |
| Southeast | .92 | .98 | .84 | 1.02 | .89 | .83 | .72 | .76 |
| South | .96 | 1.03 | .86 | 1.06 | .96 | .78 | .81 | 1.19 |

Region groupings: North and East (New England, Mid-Atlantic, Great Lakes, Northeast, North Central); West (Plains, Transmississippi, Mountains, Far West, Transplains); South (Southwest, Southeast).

way budgets in relation to population may reflect the diffusion of population throughout the western states, as well as the difficult terrain that roads must traverse. The natural-resource spending of western states could reflect programs to develop water resources, forestry, and recreational opportunities. The high spending for education in the West reflects the tendency to rely heavily on state funds for the support of public elementary and secondary schools. In addition, the large educational expenditures may also be the product of the well-developed systems of public higher education.

In the fields that account for the bulk of state spending per capita, i.e., education, highways, public welfare, and health and hospitals, southern regions show no consistent deviations from national averages. However, the southern regions score consistently low on state spending for public safety. This finding is consistent with the heavy emphasis upon local control of law enforcement which is found throughout the South and which produces strong county sheriffs and extensive systems of county prisons and work camps.

Along with these regional patterns, there are, nevertheless, marked variations in the expenditures of neighboring states. Table VI–3 shows that Vermont scores in the highest quartile of total expenditures per

**TABLE VI–3**

Total Expenditures per Capita, by States and Regions, 1962[a]

| *Regions* | *Expenditures per Capita* |
| --- | --- |
| NEW ENGLAND | |
| Maine | $163.19 |
| New Hampshire | 151.71 |
| Vermont | 255.10 |
| Massachusetts | 159.58 |
| Rhode Island | 169.71 |
| Connecticut | 182.12 |
| MID-ATLANTIC | |
| New York | 176.46 |
| New Jersey | 110.47 |
| Pennsylvania | 145.92 |
| Maryland | 179.28 |
| Delaware | 246.53 |
| SOUTHEAST | |
| Virginia | 141.56 |
| West Virginia | 180.73 |
| North Carolina | 157.52 |
| South Carolina | 141.80 |
| Georgia | 156.20 |

TABLE VI–3 (Continued)

| Regions | Expenditures per Capita |
| --- | --- |
| SOUTHEAST (Continued) | |
| Florida | 135.79 |
| Kentucky | 209.25 |
| Tennessee | 142.97 |
| Alabama | 164.19 |
| Mississippi | 168.34 |
| Arkansas | 155.14 |
| Louisiana | 251.74 |
| GREAT LAKES | |
| Ohio | 130.34 |
| Indiana | 144.87 |
| Illinois | 131.33 |
| Michigan | 195.87 |
| Wisconsin | 168.92 |
| PLAINS | |
| Minnesota | 182.76 |
| Iowa | 161.25 |
| Missouri | 140.61 |
| North Dakota | 214.29 |
| South Dakota | 186.57 |
| Nebraska | 125.49 |
| Kansas | 160.06 |
| MOUNTAINS | |
| Montana | 196.43 |
| Wyoming | 283.69 |
| Colorado | 192.13 |
| Idaho | 188.46 |
| Utah | 208.60 |
| SOUTHWEST | |
| Oklahoma | 203.64 |
| Texas | 137.21 |
| New Mexico | 238.68 |
| Arizona | 205.45 |
| FAR WEST | |
| Washington | 249.62 |
| Oregon | 221.18 |
| Nevada | 277.06 |
| California | 218.30 |

*The states are displayed here in regional demarcation 2.

capita, while most states of its region score low. In the South, Kentucky and Louisiana score in the highest quartile of total expenditures, while Florida scores in the lowest quartile. In the Southwest, more than $100 per capita separate the spending of the neighboring states of Texas and New Mexico. Table VI–4 indicates the degree of uniformity that exists in the expenditures of states in each region. It lists the regional coefficients of variability (i.e., the standard deviation divided by the mean of each region's expenditures). *Low coefficients indicate high uniformity in spending.*

States in the Far West have shown the greatest uniformity in expenditures during recent years. The coefficients of variability for this area are .10 to .14 for the 1957–1965 period. Among regions with more than ten states, Transplains and Southeast have shown the greatest homogeneity in spending. States of some regions show great variety in spending. Even small regional groups (*e.g.,* the five states of the Mid-Atlantic) have coefficients as high as .41.

When the coefficients of variability for each region are compared with the coefficients for the nation as a whole, they provide some support for the notion that regional norms influence the level of state spending. Throughout the 1903–1965 period, coefficients generally indicate greater uniformity of spending at the regional level than in the nation as a whole. The relative uniformity of regional spending levels suggests that budget-makers are more likely to follow the spending examples of neighboring states (as perhaps other officials in the state government follow the examples of their neighbors in taxation and levels of public services) than they are to look toward the activity of "national leaders." This finding complements the discovery of regionalism in the "states of reference" nominated by the state budget officers who are mentioned in the introduction to this chapter. It appears that state officials judge their own performance in the light of what their neighbors are doing. State officials often judge that their regional partners must meet economic and social problems that are most similar to their own. When moved by a sense of following leadership, state officials probably view the regional leader (rather than the national leader) as representing the target of their own development. Regional neighbors are likely to have similar service and spending levels; thus, following a leader is less demanding within regions than between regions.

## REGIONAL EXPENDITURES AND THE CORRELATES OF EXPENDITURES

Despite differences in spending levels, the major factors relating to spending are similar in almost every region. Table VI–5 indicates the degree to which expenditures in each region respond to items that influence state expenditures throughout the nation. The table lists the ratios be-

## TABLE VI-4

### Coefficients of Variability for Total State Expenditures per Capita, by Region

| | | 1965 | 1962 | 1957 | 1952 | 1947 | 1942 | 1939 | 1929 | 1924 | 1918 | 1913 | 1903 |
|---|---|---|---|---|---|---|---|---|---|---|---|---|---|
| North | North and East | .27 | .23 | .25 | .29 | .18 | .17 | .20 | .44 | .25 | .30 | .29 | .41 |
| New England | | .18 | .21 | .18 | .05 | .11 | .14 | .06 | .44 | .15 | .22 | .24 | .40 |
| Mid-Atlantic | | .41 | .29 | .35 | .42 | .17 | .24 | .27 | .45 | .27 | .26 | .17 | .16 |
| Great Lakes | | .18 | .18 | .21 | .22 | .24 | .13 | .26 | .26 | .30 | .33 | .38 | .24 |
| Northeast | | .22 | .23 | .23 | .06 | .13 | .13 | .14 | .41 | .15 | .31 | .24 | .41 |
| North Central | | .20 | .18 | .19 | .21 | .17 | .14 | .27 | .36 | .43 | .32 | .35 | .26 |
| Plains | | .21 | .18 | .18 | .20 | .10 | .15 | .26 | .38 | .46 | .34 | .37 | .29 |
| Transmississippi | West | .25 | .21 | .24 | .23 | .30 | .23 | .26 | .38 | .43 | .37 | .46 | .75 |
| Mountains | | .23 | .19 | .19 | .14 | .11 | .08 | .17 | .34 | .33 | .24 | .19 | .21 |
| Far West | | .10 | .11 | .14 | .11 | .27 | .15 | .18 | .46 | .43 | .41 | .55 | .38 |
| Transplains | | .17 | .15 | .18 | .15 | .20 | .12 | .17 | .36 | .38 | .31 | .41 | .39 |
| Southwest | South | .27 | .22 | .28 | .25 | .35 | .32 | .20 | .33 | .36 | .52 | .43 | .50 |
| Southeast | | .16 | .20 | .26 | .25 | .19 | .30 | .34 | .22 | .19 | .27 | .33 | .43 |
| South | | .25 | .21 | .29 | .33 | .22 | .31 | .39 | .40 | .42 | .31 | .44 | .41 |
| U.S. | | .27 | .23 | .26 | .28 | .28 | .27 | .32 | .41 | .44 | .43 | .45 | .50 |

tween actual spending in each region and the level of spending estimated for each region by the nationwide model of the expenditure system for 1962. Twelve of the fourteen ratios in Table VI–5 are within 3 per cent

TABLE VI–5

Ratios of Actual Total Spending per Capita to Spending Estimated on Basis of 48-State Regression Model, by Region, 1962

| Region | | Ratios |
|--------|--|--------|
| North | | .99 |
| New England | | .99 |
| Mid-Atlantic | North | 1.01 |
| Great Lakes | and | 1.00 |
| Northeast | East | 1.00 |
| North Central | | 1.00 |
| Plains | | 1.00 |
| Transmississippi | | 1.02 |
| Mountains | West | 1.00 |
| Far West | | 1.00 |
| Transplains | | 1.15 |
| Southwest | | .85 |
| Southeast | South | .98 |
| South | | .97 |

of perfect correspondence between actual and estimated expenditures. In no case does the spending of a region vary by more than 15 per cent from the spending estimated by the 48-state model.

The applicability of the 48-state regression model to the expenditures of most regions testifies to the analytic limitations of the regional concept in state expenditures. While it is true that spending varies markedly from one region to another, these variations are consistent with variations in the factors that generally correspond with state expenditures: previous expenditures, the state percentage of state-local expenditures, and local expenditures per capita. Apparently, expenditure processes are not unique to each region; except in the Transplains and Southwest, the regions respond in the same way to the same independent variables. It is not the regions themselves but other characteristics of states that seem most useful in the explanation of interstate differences in current (1962) expenditures.

*105*

Despite the weakness of regionalism in explaining current spending, the regional concept does help in the identification and understanding of *changes* in state expenditures over the years of the twentieth century. As was found in previous chapters, the data in this chapter make it clear that previous expenditures exercise considerable influence over current expenditures. The data of Table VI–6, which show regional expenditures as percentages of national expenditures, indicate that regions currently above or below national averages in spending have tended to retain such status through most decades of the twentieth century. Yet there have been significant instances of change in the spending positions of certain regions. Up to the time of World War II, states in three of the northeastern regions (New England, Mid-Atlantic, and Northeast) tended to spend at levels 10 to 30 per cent above the national average. In more recent years, however, states in these regions have tended to spend below the national average. In a reverse tendency, the states of the Southwest spent below the national average prior to World War I, but within the last decade they have reached a level of spending 18 per cent above the national average. States in the South and Southeast have been low spenders throughout the century, but since World War II they have shown considerable increases relative to the national average.

Two explanations may account for the downward shift of states in the Northeast: it may reflect either a relative lack of innovation in state government programs or a continuing vitality of local governments. The original settlers of northern colonies brought a strong local government orientation with them from the Old World, and their descendants have retained this tradition as evidenced in high local tax rates and a continuing respect for local autonomy. However, local authorities in the New England states currently show lower-than-average government spending per capita. Thus, it appears that the relative down-turn in state spending in that region reflects a general tendency of government officials to fall behind nationwide rates of development.

In the Southwest, the sharp increase in state spending after 1913 probably reflects the political maturation of such new states as Oklahoma, Arizona, and New Mexico. The earlier spending figures for these states represent the budgets of territorial governments with small populations. As populations and governmental structures of these states increased in size, they showed marked increases in spending relative to the national average.

The recent increases in spending by states in the South and Southeast has not brought them to the level of the national average, but it has brought them about three-fourths of the distance that separated them from the national average in 1903. To a large extent, the narrowing of

## TABLE VI-6

### Mean Expenditures per Capita of States in Each Region as Percentages of National Means

| | 1965 | 1962 | 1957 | 1952 | 1947 | 1942 | 1939 | 1929 | 1924 | 1918 | 1913 | 1903 |
|---|---|---|---|---|---|---|---|---|---|---|---|---|
| North | 1.08 | .93 | .95 | .91 | .97 | 1.00 | 1.11 | 1.04 | 1.04 | 1.11 | 1.15 | 1.10 |
| New England | .95 | .99 | 1.04 | .85 | 1.08 | 1.03 | 1.11 | 1.20 | 1.12 | 1.37 | 1.33 | 1.36 |
| Mid-Atlantic | .97 | .95 | .96 | 1.04 | .92 | 1.03 | 1.15 | 1.12 | 1.13 | .98 | 1.18 | 1.03 |
| Great Lakes | .86 | .85 | .85 | .84 | .90 | .95 | 1.06 | .76 | .87 | .94 | .89 | .88 |
| Northeast | .89 | .93 | .95 | .83 | 1.03 | 1.00 | 1.11 | 1.11 | 1.08 | 1.24 | 1.25 | 1.28 |
| North Central | .90 | .89 | .89 | .90 | .87 | .94 | .96 | .90 | 1.03 | .95 | .91 | .87 |
| Plains | .93 | .92 | .94 | .94 | .85 | .94 | .89 | 1.00 | 1.14 | .96 | .93 | .88 |
| Transmississippi | 1.13 | 1.10 | 1.12 | 1.15 | 1.13 | 1.14 | 1.11 | 1.11 | 1.21 | 1.17 | 1.11 | 1.16 |
| Mountains | 1.28 | 1.18 | 1.15 | 1.18 | 1.23 | 1.26 | 1.24 | 1.11 | 1.15 | 1.40 | 1.30 | 1.30 |
| Far West | 1.32 | 1.33 | 1.35 | 1.44 | 1.46 | 1.39 | 1.41 | 1.40 | 1.64 | 1.40 | 1.53 | 1.79 |
| Transplains | 1.30 | 1.24 | 1.26 | 1.29 | 1.36 | 1.33 | 1.29 | 1.25 | 1.34 | 1.38 | 1.32 | 1.42 |
| Southwest | 1.11 | 1.08 | 1.18 | 1.17 | 1.18 | 1.12 | 1.05 | 1.02 | .96 | 1.10 | .79 | .77 |
| Southeast | .88 | .92 | .87 | .88 | .82 | .75 | .67 | .77 | .59 | .56 | .64 | .61 |
| South | .93 | .96 | .93 | .97 | .84 | .80 | .77 | .84 | .69 | .63 | .70 | .65 |

Region groupings: North and East, West, South.

the gap between low and high spenders noted in Chapter III has reflected great relative increases in the spending of southern states. The factors involved in these increases may include federal aid and social and economic developments. Many federal programs give disproportionate assistance to poor states, and the southern states have taken advantage of these opportunities. Moreover, the economic progress of the South has added both resources and the desire among Southerners for improved services. Although Chapter IV notes the existence of negative relationships between changes in state spending and the levels of economic development for the 1962–1965 period, this relationship might be reversed where economic development is particularly great and long-lasting. Between 1940 and 1962, per capita personal income increased by 298 per cent throughout the United States; but it increased by 387 per cent in the region labeled here as South and by 404 per cent in the Southeast. Although personal income levels in the South still rank below the national average, no other region has shown comparable advancement in the past three decades.

## SUMMARY

There are clear regional patterns in spending in the American states. States in the western regions generally spend at levels above the national average, while those in the Northeast spend below the average in several fields of service. Southern states currently spend at levels very close to average.

The regional concept not only points to one factor that helps to distinguish high and low spenders today, but it assists in other phases of expenditure analysis. By comparing coefficients of variability computed regionally and nationally at several points throughout this century, it is possible to find evidence for regional norms in state spending. Furthermore, the evidence of changes in regional spending levels, compared to national averages, points to some basic alterations in American state governments: states in the South and Southwest have shown considerable increases in their spending positions, while states in the Northeast have stagnated in recent years.

These patterns of change may reflect the operation of cementing characteristics that help to align the current levels of spending in the various regions. These characteristics are: common levels of economic needs and resources among regional neighbors, similar governmental characteristics, and the tendency of state officials to look toward their neighbors when they seek norms to guide their own activity.

Although the notion of regional affiliation helps in the explanation of why some states spend more than others, the utility of the regional concept is limited in the explanation of current spending levels. Despite spending similarities among neighboring states, it is apparent that these differences in spending levels relate to differences in characteristics that influence spending generally. A test for 1962 with a regression equation employing the independent variables that are proven to be strong correlates nationally found that these characteristics relate to expenditures on a regional basis in about the same way as they relate to expenditures of individual states across the country. Thus, it is evident that regions do not harbor wholly different spending processes. Much of the explanation for high- (or low-) spending regions lies in the consistently high (or low) scores of their states on the items of previous expenditures, state shares of state-local spending, and local expenditures per capita.

# CHAPTER VII

# Government Expenditures and Public Services*

IN MUCH of the literature that examines the subject of state and/or local government expenditures in the United States, there is an explicit or implicit assumption that the real nugget of inquiry is the nature of public services provided by each jurisdiction. The alleged spending-service equation may reflect either of two causal patterns: (1) spending levels may provide the wherewithal for services and, therefore, be necessarily high or low where service levels are high or low; or (2) established service levels may act as demands upon budget-makers who feel constrained to continue expenditures at levels commensurate with the service or see the efforts of past years suffer financial malnutrition. Among the studies that have attempted to explain the outputs of state and local governments by reference to political and economic characteristics, several have implicitly identified expenditures with services by using a combination of indicators of spending and indicators of services as the outputs to be explained.[1] Other studies have explicitly claimed that government expenditures reflect the "scope and character" or the "alpha and the omega" of public services.[2]

*This chapter has been adapted from the author's article "Government Services and Public Services in the American States," from the December 1967 issue of the *American Political Science Review.*

[1]Richard Dawson and James Robinson, "Interparty Competition, Economic Variables, and Welfare Policies in the American States," *Journal of Politics,* 25 (May 1963): 265–89; Thomas R. Dye, "Malapportionment and Public Policy in the States," *Journal of Politics,* 27 (August 1965): 586–601; Richard I. Hofferbert, "The Relation between Public Policy and Some Structural and Environmental Variables in the American States," *American Political Science Review,* 60 (March 1966): 73–82.
[2]See, respectively, Robert C. Wood, *1400 Governments* (Garden City, N.Y.: Anchor Books, 1961), p. 35; Jesse Burkhead, *Public School Finance* (Syracuse,

However, the spending-service relationship may not exist at all. Service levels may reflect the influence of many factors, in addition to the level of current spending; and service levels must compete with many other factors in order to influence the level of state expenditures. Just as budget-makers seem to pay only marginal attention to each of the economic and governmental phenomena considered in Chapter IV, so they may pay only marginal attention to the supporters of individual services.

It is no easy task to go beneath the assumed spending-service relationship. The greatest difficulty lies in measuring the levels of public services in the states. Concepts of quality and quantity appear to be specific for each field of service and may be said to vary with the peculiar characteristics of each state which affect citizens' needs for each type of service. Despite the risks, this chapter undertakes some initial, awkward steps in the direction of measuring service levels. Because of technical problems that preclude the assessment of the services supported by *state agencies, per se,* it considers the spending and service levels of state and local governments within each state. For this reason, the findings stand somewhat aside from the prevailing discussion of state government expenditures. Nevertheless, the findings should contribute to an understanding of the context in which state government expenditures operate. And the results certainly temper the author's initial supposition that by examining expenditures he was *sotto voce* examining public services.

In assessing the relationship between spending and services, this chapter first defines static relationships between measures of spending and measures of public services. Second, it examines relationships over time in an attempt to discern whether increases in government expenditures are likely to bring about increases in the quality or quantity of public services.

## TECHNIQUES

One of the first problems encountered in the analysis of public services is the identification of services that are likely to respond to the expenditures of specific government units. In part, this is the problem of Morton Grodzins' marble cake. His view is that there are no major services that are solely the product of any one government level.[3] Rather, local, state, and federal agencies share in the planning, financing, staffing, and directing of prominent domestic services. This is certainly true in the major

---

N.Y.: Syracuse University Press, 1964), p. 50; and Philip H. Burch, Jr., *Highway Revenue and Expenditure Policy in the United States* (New Brunswick, N.J.: Rutgers University Press, 1962), p. 34.

[3]Morton Grodzins, "American Political Parties and the American System," *Western Political Quarterly,* 13 (December 1960): 974–98.

categories of state and local services. However, in several fields of service, it is possible to go beyond Grodzins' concept and note that they are the products of private efforts as well as of the activities of local, state, and federal governments. For example, officials concerned with education, public welfare, health and hospitals, and natural resources seem likely to adjust their own services, in part, to the programs of private institutions within their jurisdiction.

Because of the public-private marble cake, it is virtually impossible to obtain measures of public services that are solely the outputs of particular governments. In order to cope with this difficulty, this study examines measures of services provided *within* each state. It establishes the connections between these service indicators and the measures of combined state and local government expenditures; and it evaluates these expenditure-service relationships in the light of measures relating to federal aid, private economic activity, and other elements likely to influence services.

In this analysis, three measures of expenditures are considered likely to have influence upon public services. They are measured for both 1957 and 1962, as are the other independent variables. The three measures are:

    (a)  Combined state and local general expenditures per capita;[4]

    (b)  Combined state and local general expenditures per $1,000 of personal income; and

    (c)  Combined state and local general expenditures for each major function as a percentage of total general expenditures.

Each of these measures is calculated for expenditures in the major fields of education, highways, public welfare, health and hospitals, natural resources (agriculture, fish and game, forestry and parks), and public safety. Variable *a* measures the money spent in relation to the population served by state services. Variable *b* measures spending in relation to economic resources. As such, it indicates the effort displayed by state and local governments in supporting the different fields of service. Variable *c* measures the relative success enjoyed by each field of service in competition with other services for government expenditures.[5] If the level of government spending actually reflects the quality or quantity of public services, then each of these spending measures should show positive relationships with service indicators.

In addition to these measures of spending, 18 other independent variables were examined for having possible influence upon the nature of

---

[4]"General expenditures" include all state spending for each major category except for insurance trust funds. The year 1962 was selected for all variables because of the data present in the *Census of Governments, 1962.*

[5]See James A. Maxwell, *Financing State and Local Governments* (Washington: Brookings Institution, 1965), chapt. 2.

public services. After preliminary analysis, the following were selected for more thorough treatment:

(d) Federal aid, i.e., federal payments as a percentage of state and local spending for each service;

(e) Number of state and local employees per 10,000 population;

(f) Average salary of state and local employees;

(g) Percentage of state and local general revenue originating at sources other than local governments prior to intergovernmental transfers;

(h) Per capita personal income; and

(i) population.

Variable *d* measures an outside source of money that might influence the nature of services within each state. Variables *e* and *f* measure the size and rewards of administrative units. Presumably, these features might independently influence services without regard for expenditures. Variable *g* measures the centralization in state-local relationships.[6] The degree of centralization may influence the nature of services provided or the efficiency with which expenditures affect services. Variables *h* and *i* are economic measures that relate strongly to other measures of economic activity;[7] they indicate the base of resources from which state and local governments and private groups draw in order to provide services.[8]

---

[6]Besides the state government, the principal non-local source of state-local revenue is the federal government. A high score on variable *g* indicates centralization because most federal contributions to local governments funnel through state agencies.

[7]See Harvey S. Perloff *et al., Regions, Resources, and Economic Growth* (Baltimore: Johns Hopkins University Press, 1960), chaps. 1–3.

[8]Variables considered, but not retained, were:

(1) Percentage of per capita personal income paid in taxes to state and local governments;

(2) Percentage of state and local general revenue originating at the state level prior to intergovernmental transfers;

(3) Percentage of state and local general revenue allocated to the state level after tax collections and intergovernmental transfers;

(4) Percentage of local general revenue received from the state;

(5) Voter turnout in state elections;

(6) The David-Eisenberg measure of apportionment equity in state legislatures;

(7) A measure of party competition derived from Ranney's index of Democratic party strength;

(8) Number of local governments per 10,000 population;

(9) Percentage of population living in urban areas;

(10) Percentage of labor force employed in manufacturing;

(11) Value added by manufacturing, per capita.

Variables 1–3 of this list were dropped because they reflect the same phenomena as independent variable *g*. Variables 4–7 were dropped because they fail to show strong relationships with either government expenditures or public services. Variables 8–11 were dropped because they reflect the same phenomena as independent variables *h* and *i*.

Coefficients of simple correlation (Pearson's $r$) indicate the strength of simple relationships between each measure of spending and measure of service. Yet coefficients of simple correlation do not indicate if the spending measures have independent relationships to public services. The problem of independence would occur, for example, if variables $a$–$c$ showed positive relationships to public services only because variables $d$–$i$ have stronger positive relationships to both the measures of spending and the measures of services. Partial correlation techniques, controlling for variables $d$–$i$, provide a test for the independence of relationships between spending and services.[9]

Sixty-four variables measure various aspects of public-service quality or quantity within each state. Some variables measure the amount of benefits or services provided per client. Some indicate the units of service in relation to the total population of the state. Some measure the incidence of beneficiaries among the people likely to use a service. Still others express the rate at which a service is performed. Other variables assess services by the frequency with which the state population chooses to employ programs. Finally, some assess services indirectly by measuring the continued existence of phenomena that government activities are designed to control. The full title of each measure of service and its source are listed in the Appendix (see pp. 159–66).

While gathering the data on service levels, an effort was made to obtain measurements as close as possible to 1962 for the static analysis and as close as possible to 1957 for the analysis of change. In each case, it is assumed that the recorded data provide reasonably accurate indications of fact. It is recognized, however, that the quality of the data may occasionally disappoint the author's hopes. For comments on the quality of specific measurements, the reader is referred to the sources noted in the Appendix. Since part of the analysis employs data from 1957, prior to Alaskan and Hawaiian statehood, only 48 states are included.

## FINDINGS: STATIC RELATIONSHIPS BETWEEN EXPENDITURES AND SERVICES

The expenditure-service linkage does not appear to be strong. The coefficients of simple correlation reported in Table VII–1 show that 36 of the service measures (56 per cent) have relationships with *at least one* of the expenditure measures which is strong enough to be statistically

[9] For an illustration of this technique, see Dye, "Malapportionment." Also see Hubert Blalock, *Social Statistics* (New York: McGraw-Hill Book Co., 1960), chapt. 19.

## TABLE VII-1

### Coefficients of Simple and Partial Correlation between Measures of Spending and Services, 1962[a]

| Services | Simple Correlation Spending Measures | | | Partial Correlation[b] Spending Measures | | |
|---|---|---|---|---|---|---|
| | a | b | c | a | b | c |
| **EDUCATION** | | | | | | |
| teacher-pupil ratio (48) | .41* | −.01 | −.08 | .23 | .16 | −.02 |
| teachers with B.A. degree (49) | .00 | .08 | .29* | −.05 | .03 | .29 |
| teachers with M.A. degree (50) | .42* | .06 | .35* | .24 | .27 | .35* |
| pupils in vocational education (51) | −.20 | .33* | .12 | −.05 | −.05 | .04 |
| pupils in school lunch program (52) | −.35* | .37* | .08 | .11 | .12 | .10 |
| persons in vocational rehabilitation (53) | −.39* | −.07 | −.07 | −.34* | −.38* | −.11 |
| persons completing vocational rehabilitation (54) | −.54* | −.15 | −.05 | −.38* | −.43* | −.04 |
| school attendance (55) | .09 | −.01 | .06 | −.02 | −.14 | −.06 |
| length of school term (56) | .17 | −.21 | .01 | −.04 | −.06 | .09 |
| population per school district (57) | −.22 | −.18 | −.11 | −.25 | −.20 | −.07 |
| 9th-graders who later complete high school (58) | .25 | −.30* | .15 | −.16 | −.22 | −.23 |
| mental exam success (59) | .65* | .08 | .16 | .40* | .20 | .17 |
| M.A.'s conferred (60) | .18 | .14 | .00 | .02 | .04 | −.03 |
| Ph.D.'s conferred (61) | .39* | −.03 | .25 | .17 | .17 | .28 |
| college enrollment (62) | .07 | .09 | −.05 | −.05 | −.04 | −.08 |
| state college enrollment of state inhabitants (63) | .05 | .09 | −.05 | −.05 | −.02 | −.07 |
| **HIGHWAYS** | | | | | | |
| total road mileage (64) | .41* | .44* | .47* | .18 | .07 | .25 |
| rural road mileage (65) | −.34* | −.27 | −.18 | .07 | −.07 | .11 |
| urban road mileage (66) | .43* | .57* | .57* | .28 | .25 | .27 |
| % of farms on paved roads (67) | −.04 | −.21 | −.14 | .23 | .32* | .26 |
| 4- and 6-lane roads (68) | −.25 | −.25 | −.27 | −.09 | −.13 | −.21 |
| total interstate mileage (69) | .73* | .59* | .46* | .37* | .25 | .21 |
| % of interstate mileage completed (70) | .77* | .60* | .56* | .51* | .43* | .40* |
| % of interstate mileage in progress (71) | −.34* | −.45* | −.39* | −.04 | −.01 | −.02 |
| motor vehicle deaths (72) | −.40* | −.55* | −.47* | .01 | .04 | −.11 |

**TABLE VII-1** (Continued)

| Services | Simple Correlation Spending Measures | | | Partial Correlation[b] Spending Measures | | |
|---|---|---|---|---|---|---|
| | a | b | c | a | b | c |
| **PUBLIC WELFARE** | | | | | | |
| OAA recipients (74) | −.02 | −.07 | −.18 | −.13 | −.07 | −.11 |
| MAA recipients (75) | −.08 | −.10 | −.14 | −.06 | −.07 | −.08 |
| AFDC recipients (76) | .21 | −.07 | .02 | .24 | .27 | .29 |
| AB recipients (77) | .00 | −.07 | .01 | −.05 | −.04 | −.03 |
| APTD recipients (78) | .29* | .17 | .17 | .26 | .23 | .26 |
| OAA payment per recipient (79) | .36* | .01 | .02 | .53* | .50* | .47* |
| AFDC payment per recipient (80) | .21 | −.19 | −.13 | .41* | .35* | .38* |
| AB payment per recipient (81) | .37* | −.03 | .04 | .56* | .52* | .54* |
| APTD payment per recipient (82) | .18 | −.07 | .02 | .25 | .16 | .24 |
| child welfare recipients (83) | .08 | .14 | .06 | .13 | .14 | .09 |
| **HEALTH AND HOSPITALS** | | | | | | |
| number of hospital beds (84) | .24 | −.16 | .04 | .06 | −.04 | −.07 |
| number of hospital bassinets (85) | .00 | −.07 | −.33* | .06 | −.03 | −.10 |
| patients in mental hospitals (86) | .07 | −.11 | −.04 | .03 | .04 | −.02 |
| patients released from mental hospitals (87) | .20 | −.15 | −.04 | −.03 | −.11 | −.16 |
| patients in hospitals for mentally retarded (88) | −.11 | −.14 | −.45* | −.13 | −.19 | −.28 |
| number of physicians (89) | .40* | −.11 | .12 | −.08 | −.11 | −.19 |
| number of dentists (90) | .33* | .23 | .33* | .20 | .21 | .26 |
| number of disabled children (91) | .19 | .05 | .14 | .16 | .16 | .14 |
| white infant death rate (92) | .08 | −.14 | .17 | −.16 | −.11 | −.08 |
| non-white infant death rate (93) | .04 | −.15 | −.15 | −.13 | −.16 | −.22 |

TABLE VII-1 (Continued)

| Services | Simple Correlation Spending Measures | | | Partial Correlation[b] Spending Measures | | |
|---|---|---|---|---|---|---|
| | a | b | c | a | b | c |
| NATURAL RESOURCES | | | | | | |
| cooperative extension agents (94) | .25 | .49* | .35* | .50* | .52* | .39* |
| agricultural researchers (95) | .62* | .65* | .54* | .52* | .49* | .35* |
| soil conservation acreage (97) | −.47* | −.33* | −.37* | −.36* | −.28 | −.30* |
| mapped conservation acreage (98) | −.41* | −.37* | −.36* | −.08 | −.08 | −.10 |
| land in Agricultural Conservation Program (99) | −.07 | .03 | −.06 | .13 | .17 | .04 |
| state-park acreage (100) | .43* | .39* | .27 | .20 | .15 | .03 |
| state-park acreage per visitor (101) | .16 | .13 | .08 | .09 | .11 | .06 |
| number of state-park visitors (102) | .18 | .15 | .14 | .15 | .09 | .07 |
| fishing licenses sold (103) | .52* | .60* | .54* | .42* | .41* | .34* |
| hunting licenses sold (104) | .49* | .58* | .48* | .40* | .40* | .29 |
| PUBLIC SAFETY[c] | | | | | | |
| murder offenses (105) | .26 | .10 | .11 | −.33* | −.30* | −.37* |
| rape offenses (106) | −.37* | −.28* | −.23 | −.02 | .00 | −.05 |
| robbery offenses (107) | −.43* | −.34* | −.40* | −.01 | −.02 | −.06 |
| assault offenses (108) | −.11 | −.21 | −.27 | −.18 | −.18 | −.32* |
| burglary offenses (109) | −.51* | −.48* | −.43* | −.22 | −.25 | −.29 |
| larceny offenses (110) | −.65* | −.59* | −.43* | −.42* | −.39* | −.38* |
| auto theft offenses (111) | −.67* | −.60* | −.54* | −.38* | −.38* | −.41* |
| paroles (112) | .20 | .22 | .16 | .22 | .21 | .10 |
| parole success (113) | −.12 | −.12 | −.16 | −.02 | .00 | −.11 |

*Significant at the .05 level.

[a] For the definitions of spending measures *a-c*, see above, p. 112; for the definitions of service measures, see Appendix, pp. 159–66.

[b] Variables *d-i* are controlled.

[c] The figures pertaining to crime are inverted from their usual presentation in order that they be consistent with the other service indicators. High scores on the following indicators reflect low crime rates and high public service in the field of public safety.

117

significant.[10] There is a lower incidence of significant relationships between the service measures and *all* of the three expenditure measures. Of the 192 possible relationships between spending and services in 1962, only 72 (38 per cent) are significant. Thirty-three of the spending-service relationships that are statistically significant are actually negative. Only 39 (20 per cent) of the simple relationships between spending and services are significant in the expected direction. In some cases, it appears that public officials spend at high levels in the face of low service performance. Perhaps they hope to elevate service levels at some time in the future or to prevent further declines in services.

It is possible to square coefficients of simple correlation in order to determine the percentage of variation in one variable that is explained, statistically, by variation in another variable. When the simple coefficients of Table VII–1 are squared, it is evident that only two of the spending measures (1 per cent of the total) are powerful enough to account for 50 per cent of the interstate variation in services! These findings appear for total interstate mileage and the percentage of interstate mileage completed. For all of the other service measures, it is apparent that local government expenditures fail to play a major role in their attainment.

The relationship between spending and services appears even weaker when the influence of variables *d–i* is taken into consideration. Table VII–1 also reports coefficients of partial correlation between the measures of spending and services in 1962, while controlling for measures of federal aid, administrative size and salaries, state-local centralization, and economic development. Only 20 (31 per cent) of the service measures show significant partial correlations with any of the spending measures. Of the 192 possible relationships between the three spending measures and service indicators, 45 (23 per cent) are significant, and 27 of these (14 per cent) are in the expected direction.

If government expenditures do not exert the prevailing influence upon the quality or quantity of public services, what does explain the nature of these services? For most of the service indicators considered here, the question must remain unanswered. For only 20 of the service indicators (31 per cent) does the combination of one of the spending measures and all variables *d–i* account for at least 50 per cent of the interstate variation in services. These are the service indicators having a coefficient of multiple determination ($R^2$) of at least .50. The remaining 44 service indicators respond primarily to elements not considered in the present study. Table VII–2 shows coefficients of partial correlation

[10]Because the 48 states are not a random sample, the common tests for significance are not, strictly speaking, applicable. They will be used, however, to provide an arbitrary indication of relationships that appear "sizable."

*118*

TABLE VII–2

Coefficients of Partial Correlation between Independent Variables and Selected Service Indicators, 1962ᵃ

| Servicesᵇ | Spending Measuresᵇ | | | Independent Variables | | | | | |
|---|---|---|---|---|---|---|---|---|---|
| | a | b | c | d Federal Aid | e State-Local Employees | f Average Salary | g Centralization | h Personal Income | i Population |
| **EDUCATION** | | | | | | | | | |
| teacher-pupil ratio (48) | .23 | | | −.07 | .15 | −.21 | −.51* | .25 | −.41* |
| teacher-pupil ratio (48) | | .16 | | −.04 | .23 | −.16 | −.50* | .26 | −.43* |
| teacher-pupil ratio (48) | | | −.02 | .01 | .41* | −.07 | −.48* | .21 | −.47* |
| pupils in school lunch program (52) | .11 | | | −.02 | .02 | −.23 | .17 | −.40* | .11 |
| pupils in school lunch program (52) | | .12 | | −.02 | .03 | −.24 | .16 | −.20 | .12 |
| pupils in school lunch program (52) | | | .10 | −.01 | .15 | −.23 | .20 | −.39* | .10 |
| persons completing vocational rehabilitation (54) | −.38* | | | .16 | .04 | .02 | .47* | .12 | −.04 |
| persons completing vocational rehabilitation (54) | | −.43* | | .17 | .03 | .03 | .50* | −.23 | −.06 |
| mental exam success (59) | .40* | | | .05 | −.05 | −.04 | −.58* | .11 | −.37* |
| mental exam success (59) | | .20 | | .11 | .14 | .11 | −.54* | .18 | −.40* |
| mental exam success (59) | | | .17 | .12 | .34* | .24 | −.52* | .08 | −.44* |

TABLE VII–2 (Continued)

| Services[b] | Spending Measures[b] | | | Independent Variables | | | | | |
|---|---|---|---|---|---|---|---|---|---|
| | *a* | *b* | *c* | Federal Aid *d* | State-Local Employees *e* | Average Salary *f* | Centralization *g* | Personal Income *h* | Population *i* |
| **HIGHWAYS** | | | | | | | | | |
| total interstate mileage (69) | .37* | | | .24 | .46* | .05 | .09 | –.13 | .00 |
| total interstate mileage (69) | | .25 | | .29 | .52* | .05 | .05 | –.02 | –.03 |
| total interstate mileage (69) | | | .21 | .31* | .58* | .09 | .08 | –.09 | –.02 |
| % of interstate mileage completed (70) | .51* | | | .09 | .16 | –.07 | .09 | .21 | –.32* |
| % of interstate mileage completed (70) | | .43* | | .14 | .24 | –.05 | .05 | .35* | –.34* |
| % of interstate mileage completed (70) | | | .40* | .17 | .37* | .05 | .12 | .25 | –.31* |
| motor vehicle deaths (72) | .01 | | | –.31* | –.43* | .07 | –.19 | .32* | –.09 |
| motor vehicle deaths (72) | | .04 | | –.32* | –.45* | .07 | –.19 | .32* | –.09 |
| motor vehicle deaths (72) | | | –.11 | –.26 | –.46* | .03 | –.23 | .31* | –.11 |

TABLE VII-2 (Continued)

| Services[b] | Spending Measures[b] | | | Independent Variables | | | | | |
| | a | b | c | Federal Aid (d) | State-Local Employees (e) | Average Salary (f) | Centralization (g) | Personal Income (h) | Population (i) |
|---|---|---|---|---|---|---|---|---|---|
| **PUBLIC WELFARE** | | | | | | | | | |
| OAA recipients (74) | −.13 | | | .16 | .51* | −.06 | .27 | .34* | −.25 |
| OAA recipients (74) | | −.07 | | .16 | .50* | −.07 | .26 | .32* | −.25 |
| OAA recipients (74) | | | −.11 | .17 | .49* | −.08 | .26 | .34* | −.25 |
| AFDC recipients (76) | .24 | | | .14 | −.23 | .40* | .30* | .38* | −.03 |
| AFDC recipients (76) | | .27 | | .14 | −.23 | .42* | .28 | .41* | −.04 |
| AFDC recipients (76) | | | .29 | .12 | −.18 | .43* | .31* | .38* | −.04 |
| OAA payment per recipient (79) | .53* | | | −.31* | .19 | .26 | −.38* | −.11 | −.17 |
| OAA payment per recipient (79) | | .50* | | −.31* | .21 | .30* | −.39* | −.01 | −.16 |
| OAA payment per recipient (79) | | | .47* | −.34* | .31* | .33* | −.35* | −.13 | −.15 |
| AFDC payment per recipient (80) | .41* | | | −.36* | −.06 | .46* | −.43* | −.10 | −.35* |
| AFDC payment per recipient (80) | | .35* | | −.35* | −.03 | .48* | −.43* | −.04 | −.34* |
| AFDC payment per recipient (80) | | | .38* | −.38* | .04 | .50* | −.41* | −.12 | −.35* |
| AB payment per recipient (81) | .56* | | | −.17 | .15 | .23 | −.30* | .21 | −.20 |
| AB payment per recipient (81) | | .52* | | −.16 | .18 | .27 | −.32* | .29 | −.20 |
| AB payment per recipient (81) | | | .54* | −.22 | .29 | .31* | −.28 | .18 | −.20 |

TABLE VII-2 (Continued)

| Services[b] | Spending Measures[b] | | | Independent Variables | | | | | |
|---|---|---|---|---|---|---|---|---|---|
| | a | b | c | Federal Aid d | State-Local Employees e | Average Salary f | Centralization g | Personal Income h | Population i |
| HEALTH AND HOSPITALS | | | | | | | | | |
| number of physicians (89) | | | −.19 | −.25 | −.21 | .09 | .11 | .33* | .15 |
| NATURAL RESOURCES | | | | | | | | | |
| cooperative extension agents (94) | .50* | | | .53* | .24 | −.36* | −.34* | −.22 | −.09 |
| cooperative extension agents (94) | | .52* | | .57* | .28 | −.32* | −.37* | −.05 | −.06 |
| cooperative extension agents (94) | | | .39* | .50* | .45* | −.26 | −.27 | −.21 | −.09 |
| agricultural researchers (95) | .52* | | | .38* | .44* | −.08 | −.24 | −.03 | −.48* |
| agricultural researchers (95) | | .49* | | .41* | .49* | .00 | −.27 | .09 | −.45* |
| agricultural researchers (95) | | | .35* | .34* | .62* | .05 | −.17 | −.07 | −.45* |
| fishing licenses sold (103) | .42* | | | .42* | .18 | .24 | −.48* | −.43* | −.32* |
| fishing licenses sold (103) | | .41* | | .44* | .22 | .30* | −.49* | −.31* | −.29 |
| fishing licenses sold (103) | | | .34* | .40* | .36* | .33* | −.43* | −.42* | −.30* |
| hunting licenses sold (104) | .40* | | | .41* | .21 | .09 | −.36* | −.26 | −.27 |
| hunting licenses sold (104) | | .40* | | .44* | .25 | .15 | −.38* | −.14 | −.25 |
| hunting licenses sold (104) | | | .29 | .39* | .39* | .19 | −.31* | −.26 | −.26 |

TABLE VII-2 (Continued)

| Services[b] | Spending Measures[c] | | | Independent Variables | | | | | |
|---|---|---|---|---|---|---|---|---|---|
| | a | b | c | Federal Aid *d* | State-Local Employees *e* | Average Salary *f* | Centralization *g* | Personal Income *h* | Population *i* |
| **PUBLIC SAFETY[c]** | | | | | | | | | |
| murder offenses (105) | −.33* | | | | .05 | .42* | −.50* | .13 | −.41* |
| murder offenses (105) | | | −.37* | | −.15 | .38* | −.54* | .14 | −.42* |
| larceny offenses (110) | −.42* | | | | −.30* | −.14 | −.38* | .05 | −.03 |
| larceny offenses (110) | | −.39* | | | −.32* | −.15 | −.37* | −.21 | −.05 |
| larceny offenses (110) | | | −.38* | | −.45* | −.27 | −.41* | .00 | −.04 |
| auto theft offenses (111) | −.38* | | | | −.10 | −.08 | −.23 | −.06 | .05 |
| auto theft offenses (111) | | −.38* | | | −.11 | −.07 | −.22 | −.29 | .03 |
| auto theft offenses (111) | | | −.41* | | −.30* | −.19 | −.29 | −.08 | .05 |

*Significant at the .05 level.

[a]Selected are those combinations of a spending measure with variables *d–i* that account for at least 50 per cent of the interstate variation in a service indicator; the partial correlations represent the relationship between an independent variable and a service indicator, while controlling for the influence of all other independent variables.

[b]See note a in Table VII–1. For the definitions of variables *d–i*, see above, p. 113.

[c]See note c in Table VII–1.

between the independent variables and each service indicator having an $R^2$ of at least .50. Measures of spending show significant positive relationships to 11 of the 25 service indicators in the table. Only with four service indicators, however, does a spending measure show a stronger positive coefficient of partial correlation than does any of the other independent variables. Spending measures show the strongest partial relationships to payments for Old Age Assistance and Aid to the Blind, agricultural researchers, and proportion of interstate mileage completed. Public-safety spending shows strong relationships to crimes of larceny and auto theft, but the direction of the relationships suggests that high crime rates lead to spending, rather than that spending acts upon the crime rate.

Measures of administrative size, state-local centralization, per capita personal income, and population show some consistent relationships to the service indicators in Table VII–2. The findings for the number of employees and for personal income suggest that relatively wealthy states with large administrative corps (relative to population) are likely to be high producers of public services. The findings about population suggest that elements generating public services are most likely to occur in states with small populations. The findings about state-local centralization indicate that a *decentralized* system seems to work in behalf of service outputs. Aside from the measures of expenditures, it is only the measures of administrative size and state-local centralization that show the strongest relationships to several measures of service. Per capita personal income shows the strongest coefficient of partial correlation only with the number of pupils in the school lunch program, and population fails to show the strongest coefficient of partial correlation with any of the service indicators.

There are several possible explanations for the general lack of close ties between current measures of government expenditures and public services. The magnitude of funds previously spent in accumulating capital facilities or in assembling a staff of a certain calibre might influence the capacity of current spending to stimulate service outputs. A state may score relatively high in certain types of highway mileage despite relatively low current spending. The market costs of services or products may vary significantly from one area to another. In the case of several programs, private expenditures may affect the service levels and result in weak relationships between government spending and the indicators considered here. Economies of large-scale operations may confound the simple relationship between spending and services. Certain characteristics of a program's clientele or of its political environment may also influence the efficiency with which money produces services. In the field of education, for example, the family background of students may be a critical ingredient in the quality of services. Where the environment supports favoritism in the hiring of personnel or in the choice of sites for new facilities, the ratio between financial inputs and outputs in desired services may be less than where "professional" criteria prevail. Measurement of such characteristics may add considerably to the present capacity to explain interstate variations in public services.

## FINDINGS: RELATIONSHIPS BETWEEN CHANGES IN SPENDING AND SERVICES

It is possible that changes in spending will exert great influence over changes in public services, despite the lack of strong relationships between current spending and the current level of services. Such phenomena as the level of private support for services, the characteristics of a program's clientele, or its political environment may remain stable over a period of several years so that increases in government spending can act upon the quality or quantity of public services.

In order to test the relationships between changes in expenditures and changes in public services, the analyses above were repeated using measures of 1957–1962 percentage change in variables *a–i* and measures of 1957–1962 percentage change for those service indicators where the data were available. The 1957–1962 period was selected to take advantage of the data collected by the Census of Governments in those years. In general, both expenditures and service levels increased slowly during the period. Presumably, the five-year span includes some of the lag that may occur between changes in spending and changes in services. Table VII–3 reports coefficients of simple and partial correlation for changes in spending and services.

The analysis of change shows even fewer relationships between spending and services than does the static analysis. Of the 45 service indicators for which measures of change are available, 13 (29 per cent) show significant simple relationships to any measure of change in spending. Of the 135 possible relationships between changes in three measures of spending and changes in services, 26 (19 per cent) are significant. Twenty of the relationships (15 per cent) are significant in the expected direction. When the influence of change in variables *d–i* is taken into account by partial correlation techniques, it is found that 11 (24 per cent) of the service measures show significant relationships to any of the spending measures. Of the 135 partial relationships between measures

TABLE VII-3

Coefficients of Simple and Partial Correlation between Measures of Change in Spending and Services, 1957–1962[a]

| Services | Simple Correlation | | | Partial Correlation[b] | | |
|---|---|---|---|---|---|---|
| | Spending Measures | | | Spending Measures | | |
| | a | b | c | a | b | c |
| EDUCATION | | | | | | |
| teacher-pupil ratio (48) | −.01 | −.13 | −.03 | −.09 | −.15 | .03 |
| pupils in vocational education (51) | −.04 | .11 | .19 | −.11 | −.09 | .05 |
| persons in vocational rehabilitation (53) | −.16 | −.19 | −.08 | −.21 | −.02 | −.02 |
| persons completing vocational rehabilitation (54) | −.03 | .04 | −.24 | .28 | −.27 | −.09 |
| 9th graders who later complete high school (58) | −.14 | −.19 | −.21 | −.32* | −.24 | −.20 |
| mental exam success (59) | −.11 | −.23 | −.24 | .21 | −.20 | −.27 |
| M.A.'s conferred (60) | −.07 | −.09 | −.11 | −.12 | −.11 | −.15 |
| Ph.D.'s conferred (61) | .06 | −.11 | −.04 | −.09 | −.15 | −.07 |
| college enrollment (62) | −.12 | −.05 | .01 | .00 | .01 | .13 |
| HIGHWAYS | | | | | | |
| total road mileage (64) | .30* | .26 | .23 | .06 | .05 | .05 |
| rural road mileage (65) | .08 | .11 | .00 | −.02 | .02 | .01 |
| urban road mileage (66) | .03 | .06 | .03 | .28 | .27 | .22 |
| 4- and 6-lane roads (68) | .13 | .07 | .20 | .05 | .05 | .14 |
| total interstate mileage (69) | −.36* | −.35* | −.36* | −.49* | −.48* | −.46* |
| % of interstate mileage completed (70) | −.43* | −.41* | −.42* | −.50* | −.49* | −.47* |
| motor vehicle deaths (72) | −.02 | .13 | .09 | .33* | .33* | .33* |

TABLE VII–3 (Continued)

| Services | Simple Correlation | | | Partial Correlation[b] | | |
|---|---|---|---|---|---|---|
| | Spending Measures | | | Spending Measures | | |
| | a | b | c | a | b | c |
| **PUBLIC WELFARE** | | | | | | |
| OAA recipients (74) | .15 | .15 | .16 | .14 | .13 | .00 |
| AFDC recipients (76) | .27 | .38* | .39* | .51* | .53* | .56* |
| AB recipients (77) | .12 | .19 | .31* | .09 | .12 | .27 |
| APTD recipients (78) | −.03 | .01 | −.02 | .12 | .13 | −.02 |
| OAA payment per recipient (79) | −.01 | .23 | .16 | .01 | .29 | .17 |
| AFDC payment per recipient (80) | .00 | .29* | .38* | .01 | .46* | .53* |
| AB payment per recipient (81) | −.06 | .13 | .18 | −.03 | .18 | .18 |
| APTD payment per recipient (82) | .30* | .08 | .17 | .29 | .04 | .20 |
| **HEALTH AND HOSPITALS** | | | | | | |
| number of hospital bassinets (85) | .32* | .31* | .28* | .38* | .37* | .33* |
| patients in mental hospitals (86) | .00 | .01 | .03 | .08 | .08 | .08 |
| number of physicians (89) | .92* | .86* | .89* | .94* | .90* | .92* |
| number of dentists (90) | .92* | .86* | .89* | .94* | .90* | .93* |
| white infant death rate (92) | .25 | .27 | .28* | .25 | .26 | .28 |
| non-white infant death rate (93) | .17 | .19 | .20 | .14 | .16 | .16 |

TABLE VII–3 (Continued)

| Services | Simple Correlation Spending Measures | | | Partial Correlation[b] Spending Measures | | |
|---|---|---|---|---|---|---|
| | a | b | c | a | b | c |
| **Natural Resources** | | | | | | |
| cooperative extension agents (94) | −.07 | −.05 | .28* | −.05 | −.07 | .18 |
| agricultural researchers (95) | −.03 | .04 | −.23 | −.05 | −.01 | −.18 |
| soil conservation acreage (97) | −.16 | −.23 | .05 | −.14 | −.20 | .08 |
| state-park acreage (100) | .38* | .38* | −.23 | .37* | .35* | −.05 |
| state-park acreage per visitor (101) | .25 | .14 | −.09 | .41* | .32* | −.26 |
| number of state-park visitors (102) | .16 | .19 | −.10 | .12 | .11 | −.24 |
| fishing licenses sold (103) | −.11 | −.04 | −.21 | −.06 | .01 | −.26 |
| hunting licenses sold (104) | .15 | .21 | −.15 | .19 | .24 | −.18 |
| **Public Safety**[c] | | | | | | |
| murder offenses (105) | .11 | .12 | .05 | .16 | .17 | .15 |
| robbery offenses (107) | .10 | .09 | .06 | .14 | .14 | .11 |
| assault offenses (108) | .01 | .07 | −.01 | .07 | .07 | .07 |
| burglary offenses (109) | .02 | .00 | .03 | .05 | .05 | .07 |
| larceny offenses (110) | .06 | .00 | .02 | −.01 | −.02 | −.07 |
| auto theft offenses (111) | .01 | −.01 | −.03 | −.01 | −.01 | −.05 |
| paroles (112) | −.08 | −.07 | −.04 | −.08 | −.07 | −.02 |

*Significant at the .05 level.
[a]See note a in Table VII–1.
[b]Changes in variables d–i are controlled.
[c]See note c in Table VII–1.

of change in spending and services, 28 (21 per cent) are significant. Twenty-one (16 per cent) of the partial correlations are significant in the expected direction.

On the basis of the existing data, it is virtually impossible to assess the elements that do influence changes in public services. The coefficients of multiple determination derived from this analysis reveal that combinations of present independent variables explain 50 per cent of the inter-state variation for only three of the service indicators! It is possible that the five-year time span built into the analysis is not long enough to allow changes in the independent variables to affect changes in public services. Or perhaps other elements subject to state-by-state measurement—besides those included in variables *a–i*—are generally influential with respect to changes in services. Or perhaps marked changes in services typically result from the fortuitous combination of elements that do not lend themselves to state-by-state measurement. For example, changes in personnel within the executive or legislative branches of state government or changes in local leadership may occur in ways that permit a sudden upsurge of service levels. The concept of *distributive lag*[11] may also help to explain the low incidence of significant correlations between measures of 1957–1962 change in spending and service levels. Presumably, there is a lag between changes in spending and changes in service levels within each state; and the nature of this lag may vary markedly (or be *distributed*) from one state to another. Such contingencies as the level of service capitalization, the quality of staff, or exigencies of the legislative process might work in favor of a relatively short or long lag in particular states. Because the period of lag is not constant, a correlation technique that examines relationships among changes between fixed points *a* and *b* might overlook some of the stimulus given to a change in services by a change in spending.

## SUMMARY AND CONCLUSIONS

In contrast to the assumptions of several authors, it is evident that the levels of state and local government spending do not exert pervasive influence upon the nature of public services. There are many weak relationships and some negative relationships between current spending and services and between changes in spending and changes in services. There are several possible reasons for the lack of expected relationships between

---

[11]See L. M. Koyck, *Distributed Lags and Investment Analysis* (Amsterdam: North-Holland Publishing Company, 1952), and M. Nerlove, *Estimation and Identification of Cobb-Douglas Production Functions* (Chicago: Rand McNally & Co., 1965), chapt. VII.

spending and services. The level of private spending or previous capitalization may affect the present measures of services enough to obscure some of the influence from current government spending; market costs may vary from one state to another; economies of scale may affect the spending-service linkage; or the nature of clientele and political environment may influence the spending-service relationship.

The present findings should temper expectations about the impact on service levels from current government spending. By themselves, however, these findings do not stand as an argument against increases in government spending. The findings are the product of gross analysis, employing the large categories of education, highways, public welfare, health and hospitals, natural resources, and public safety. The results do not mean that focused increases in spending will fail to improve particular services or institutions. Furthermore, the findings do not strike at the variety of reasons for increasing public expenditures that do not assume an early increase in services. Such reasons include the desire to keep salaries of public employees equivalent to those of people in comparable non-governmental positions and the desire to improve staff or physical plant for the sake of obtaining service improvements over the long range or for the sake of avoiding a deterioration of services. The data here only warn that gross levels of spending do not reflect service levels, and that gross increases in spending are not likely to produce early gross improvements in services.

CHAPTER VIII

# What Remains after Statistical Analysis: Unexplained Variations and Peculiarities of State Government Expenditures

A TRADITIONAL political scientist might search in vain through most of the preceding seven chapters for some signs of politics. The discussion has avoided a recitation of the names, motivations, and deeds of particular individuals or political organizations. There has been no comment about party platforms or bargains struck in smoky budget sessions. There is no conscious evaluation of the budget procedures, expenditure levels, or public services of specific state governments. Rather, the discussion has focused on statistical relationships among readily measured variables that purport to reflect phenomena of potential importance for state budgeting. The activities of real people have barely shown themselves above the data of statistical tables.

Although the quantitative emphasis of preceding chapters has been necessary in order to indicate the basic parameters of the expenditure process, the statistical relationships cannot claim to tell the whole story of state government spending. The problem is not simply that readers may take offense at the absence of commentary on the principals who are featured in most books about American state governments. Rather, the problem is that the foregoing statistical relationships ignore several ingredients of the expenditure process which appear important. In particular, the aggregate message of Chapters III to VII has three shortcomings: (1) the statistical relationships do not provide a thorough explanation of interstate variations in the measures of government spending; (2) even where statistical explanations of interstate variations are impressive in magnitude, they do not by themselves provide a satisfactory explanation of the human activity that is reflected in the numerical relationships; and (3) the statistical relationships do not illustrate (or show to be unimportant) the activities of particular individuals who are identified by perceptive individuals as being critical to certain spending decisions.

It is true that the statistical explanation of current general spending per capita is relatively thorough. As noted in Table IV–4, a combination of three variables—previous expenditures, the state percentage of state-local expenditures, and total local government expenditures per capita— accounts for 95 per cent of the interstate *differences* in total state spending per capita in 1962. However, the variables of this study are not as successful in accounting for the *magnitude* and *direction* of changes in state spending. The most powerful correlates of the percentage of change in total expenditures per capita from 1962 to 1965 account for only 50 per cent of interstate variation, and the most powerful correlates of 1962– 1965 change in absolute dollars account for only 64 per cent of interstate variation. The evidence of Chapters III and IV is persuasive in indicating the factors that are associated with the levels of spending which states have built up over the span of their existence. However, there appears to be considerable opportunity for the dynamic individual or political organization to exert influence on the nature of changes during individual budget periods; and the quantitative variables examined in this study provide no direct measurement of the activity of politically successful individuals or organizations.

Moreover, none of the strong statistical relationships provide, within themselves, an explanation of how the important independent variables affect the size of current spending or the size and direction of the change in spending experienced during a period of time. The actors who are involved in the decisions that affect these outcomes include administrators in the line agencies, officials in the central budget office or in the governor's office, and members of appropriations committees in the state legislature. In general, it is apparent that their decisions respond to the following phenomena: the level of previous spending, the magnitude of financial responsibility assigned to state agencies (as opposed to local authorities), federal aids, the nature of the tax system, the size of the state bureaucracy, and the levels of population, urbanization, and industrialization within the state. But how do specific actors respond to these influences? What behavioral patterns serve to link these governmental and economic characteristics to spending decisions? What range of activity is shown by officials working under the influence of their environment? Answers to these questions will not only infuse some political life into these pages, but they will also supplement the answer to the basic question of this book: "Why do some state governments spend more money than others?"

It is necessary to examine the actions of individual public personalities who are involved in the budget process not only because their behavior may help to illuminate some of the statistical relationships discussed in the preceding chapters, but because their formal positions assign budgeting responsibilities to them. If an analysis of state government expenditures ignored the official budget-makers, it would, by implication, suggest that they have little influence on spending decisions; such might in fact be the case, but a conclusion of this sort should not be left to implication. Indeed, this book makes no claim that individuals charged with formal spending responsibilities have little influence on the decisions that they make. While previous chapters have focused on the expenditure constraints and stimuli that seem to be generally present in the officials' environment, this chapter seeks to describe some of the openings where the participants may exert influence on spending.

## TECHNIQUES

The analytic methods used in this chapter do not continue the statistical preoccupation of Chapters III to VII. For the most part, this chapter focuses on descriptions of several budgeting processes which have been gathered by means of unstructured interviews with participants and native observers of state politics. As such, the techniques reflect the tools of the journalist as much as they show the influence of behavioral science. However, preceding the interviews, there was a selection process designed to identify spending activity that was substantially out of the ordinary. This chapter does not claim to cover a "random" sample of spending decisions; instead, it seeks to describe unusual cases, with the hope of depicting a wide range of the behaviors capable of affecting changes in state expenditures.

The spending decisions that are treated in this chapter are taken from states that showed changes in spending during the 1957–1965 period which were sharply at variance with the changes generally associated with their spending levels. These states were identified by the regression technique described in Chapter III. For each major service, each state's spending was estimated for the years 1962, 1963, and 1965 according to this formula:

$$Y = a + bX.$$

$Y$ equals the level of the state's *current* spending, for 1962, 1963, or 1965. $X$ equals the level of the state's *previous* spending, for 1957, 1961, or 1963, respectively.[1] Finally, *a* and *b* are constants that reflect the degree of change which was normal for the 48 states during the period at hand. Cases of deviant state expenditure were then found by comparing actual with estimated spending, as expressed in the following ratio:

$$\frac{\text{actual spending}}{\text{estimated spending}}.$$

When this ratio of actual to estimated spending varied from 1.00 (obtained when actual spending equals estimated spending) by at least 15 per cent, the expenditure change in a state was considered to be markedly above or below the *normal* level of change during the period. Subsequently, an effort was made to identify the phenomena likely to explain the unusual increase or unusual lethargy in spending.

To ensure accurate identification of these phenomena, the author sought the advice of officials in central budget offices, of professional political scientists of long residence in the various states, and of executives in the agencies whose budgets showed the deviations. Due to difficulties involved in traveling to many states for interviews and in establishing contacts with cooperative respondents for a task that promised to consume much of their time, the coverage of deviant cases is not complete. Fortunately, a number of officials in state agencies took considerable pains in suggesting explanations for the noticeable spurts or lags in their states' spending. Some volunteered persuasive, well-documented explanations of their recent spending patterns. Some gave generously of their time in personal conversations with the author. A reasonable effort was made in each case to check an informant's report against the explanation of other informants or with relevant "hard" data. However, it is possible that conditions not apparent to the author or to his informants had a direct impact on the spending decisions at issue. The discussions that follow should be viewed with the care that is normally associated with descriptions that attempt to abstract salient factors from complex decision processes. The reader should also realize that the following descriptions are not meant to depict discrete conditions that are likely to produce similar spending results if they occur in other states. Indeed,

[1] In keeping with the years considered in Chapter III, 1957 was chosen as the year for expenditures "previous" to 1962. In order to obtain instances of marked deviation from national patterns of change that would be recent enough to be fresh in the minds of participants and observers, two occasions of more recent spending were considered: 1961–1963 and 1963–1965. The years chosen for "previous" expenditures were two years behind "current" expenditures because of many states' use of biennial budgets. If current and previous spending years were taken from the same biennium, they would not reflect separate decision processes, and the ratios computed would not support the claim that certain environmental factors stimulated states to change their spending levels more or less than the national average.

it seems that in each case a peculiar "mixture" of factors, rather than individual ingredients acting alone, stimulated specific spending decisions.

## PECULIARITIES OF STATE SPENDING PROCESSES

Participants and observers have cited a variety of factors that have exerted an influence on spending decisions in their states during the 1957–1965 period. Prominent in their reports are peculiar economic and social conditions: the efforts of governors who have been intense in their desires to hasten or retard the rate of spending increase; the nature of relationships between members of executive and legislative branches; and agency willingness or reluctance to take advantage of new opportunities for federal grants. These conditions have little in common except the multiplicity of factors that seem to work in favor of a spurt or lag in government spending. There is an absence of single-factor explanations for the deviant cases of expenditure change. Indeed, the plurality of stimulants that are necessary to move a state's spending markedly upward or downward relative to other states may reflect the generally strong influence of incremental budgeting and nation-wide factors. It appears that many factors must work in concert—although perhaps coming together coincidentally and without a conscious moving force—in order to break the hold of the past and the measured increment on the budget-makers' sense of propriety.

### Massachusetts

Massachusetts' spending lag during the 1957–1962 period seems to reflect long-developing economic adversity, a peculiar social characteristic that softened the demand for public school funds, and a protracted revenue dispute between the legislature and several governors. The result was a 1962 level of spending considerably below that expected on the basis of the state's 1957 spending; as noted in Table III–8 (p. 50), Massachusetts' actual spending during 1962 was only 82 per cent of its estimated spending. Although the state increased its total per capita spending from $149.61 to $158.58 during the five-year period, it showed a relative decline from 109 per cent of the 48-state average in 1957 to 88 per cent of the 48-state average in 1962.

During each decade between 1920 and 1960, Massachusetts' economic growth lagged behind that of other states. The population of the Commonwealth increased by 35 per cent from 1920 to 1960, and the personal income of its citizens increased by 221 per cent; but comparable figures for the country as a whole were 69 per cent and 343 per cent. While the findings of Chapter IV indicate an inverse association between economic conditions and changes in spending, those findings were not strong enough to preclude a direct relationship between changes in economics and changes in spending within a single state. Massachusetts' example suggests that a long-developing economic lag may have an impact on the resources available for state expenditures. But economic conditions do not bear the entire weight of explaining the relative lag in Massachusetts' 1957–1962 spending. The state and local governments of the Commonwealth have remained dependent upon high-rate, controversial property taxes longer and to a greater extent than governments in other states. Massachusetts' governments received 57 per cent of their tax revenue from property taxes during 1957, while state and local governments throughout the country received only 44 per cent of their tax revenue from this source. It is not unlikely that the relatively burdensome nature of the property tax had a deterring effect upon the state's revenues and expenditures during the 1957–1962 period.

The Massachusetts legislature enacted a general sales tax in 1966, but only after a long struggle extending over the terms of several governors and including the 1957–1962 period. In each of several sessions, the governor and his spokesmen in the legislature claimed that the state government could not maintain desired standards of public service without the additional revenues that a new tax source would provide. During the campaign for the sales tax, it is reported that the administration's economists issued conservative estimates of the revenue to be produced by existing taxes; their low estimates might have helped to depress state expenditures during the late 1950's and early 1960's.

Along with its economic and fiscal problems, Massachusetts' extensive systems of private and parochial schools and colleges also worked against the normal rate of increase in expenditures between 1957 and 1962. Increased spending for education accounted for much of the 1957–1962 increase in total expenditures across the United States. But in 1962, 24 per cent of Massachusetts' elementary- and secondary-school pupils attended non-public schools, and 25 per cent of the educational institutions in the state were private; comparable figures for the nation were 17 and 15 per cent. A number of observers in Massachusetts have reported that the high incidence of reliance on private education has retarded the financial efforts that state (and local) authorities can make in behalf of public education. While the 48-state expenditures for education increased by 83 per cent between 1957 and 1962, Massachusetts' expenditures for education increased by only 61 per cent.

## Kentucky

It is possible that a fortuitous combination of political factors may come together in such a way as to permit dramatic increases in spending. An example of this situation can be seen in Kentucky between 1957 and 1962. During that period, Kentucky increased its total spending per capita from $94.60 to $209.25; the state's spending rose from 69 per cent of the 48-state average in 1957 to 116 per cent of the 48-state average in 1962. As noted in Table III–8 (see p. 50), Kentucky's 1962 spending per capita was 49 per cent above the level predicted for the state on the basis of its 1957 expenditures.

The factors that are considered to be critical in Kentucky's 1957–1962 spurt are a liberal governor committed to improvements in public services, and an independently inspired proposal in the legislature which provided a "natural" vehicle for the governor's revenue needs. Governor Bert Combs, who was from the impoverished counties in the eastern Kentucky mountains, was the first man from that area to be elected governor in many years. In contrast to what had been customary reluctance in the Governor's office, Combs favored increased taxation and spending in order to deal with the state's needs for economic development and improvements in education, highways, and other services. Apparently without the Governor's knowledge, a veterans' bonus bill was introduced into the state legislature and approved by legislators who were reluctant to vote against a device that had been previously used to boost fortunes temporarily in the impoverished state. According to some legislators, they could not vote against the bill, but they hoped that a "fiscally responsible" Governor would exercise his veto. A critical ingredient in the bill was its provision for funds: a bond issue to raise bonus money immediately, and a small and temporary sales tax to pay off the bonds. Governor Combs saw the veterans' bonus as protective cover for a new tax bill. He set out to support the bonus bill, but with a permanent 3 per cent sales tax attached to it. Whereas certain legislators had hoped to gain their constituents' support by voting for the original bonus bill that they hoped the Governor would veto, some of these same legislators found themselves unable to vote against a permanent sales tax because it came to them in a package with the bonus. On the basis of new revenues, Kentucky expenditures moved dramatically upward, especially in the fields of education, highways, and natural resources. Each major rise in spending was heralded as a boon to economic development: education would provide training to meet the demands of modern industry and prepare Kentucky children to reap the fruits of progress; highways would provide the transportation necessary for economic progress; and expenditures for natural resources would include funds to develop a state park system capable of attracting out-of-state tourists and providing employment for residents of the poor mountain counties.

## Ohio

Ohio informants cite a pattern of gubernatorial influence on expenditures that is opposite to the stimulant provided by Governor Combs of Kentucky. Per capita spending for education in Ohio increased by 12 per cent during the 1961–1963 period, but this rise was not as large as the prevalent levels of growth during the period. According to personnel in the state's Department of Education, the Governor's posture against new taxes figured prominently in their hold-the-line budgeting. The preceding Governor, Michael DiSalle, had been defeated during a campaign in which Governor James Rhodes had attacked DiSalle's record of taxation and spending. During the first years of the Rhodes administration, personnel in the line departments felt the weight of his continuing opposition to new taxes and to major increases in spending that would require new taxes.

## Alabama and Rhode Island

The cases of welfare expenditures in Alabama and Rhode Island during the 1961–1965 period illustrate the opportunities provided to state agencies by federal grants. Alabama, from 1961 to 1963, and Rhode Island, from 1963 to 1965, showed increases in state spending which were stimulated by new federal grants. The Alabama case shows a welfare department taking early advantage of a new federal program that promised a low "effort" increase in the state's welfare program. In contrast, Rhode Island's 1961–1963 period illustrates some of the elements that might deter a state from exploiting a new federal opportunity.

From 1961 to 1963, Alabama's expenditures per capita for public welfare increased by 31 per cent; this change elevated the state's welfare spending from 122 to 139 per cent of the 48-state average. The state's welfare expenditures in 1963 were 21 per cent above the level predicted on the basis of 1961 spending. In an immediate sense, the increase reflected Alabama's early acceptance of certain provisions of the 1960 amendments to the Social Security Act. When Alabama's early adoption of these federal provisions is viewed in the long-range development of welfare programs in that state, however, the 1961–1963 expenditure change appears to be a recent development in a motif that has deep roots in Alabama politics.

The move that seemed directly responsible for Alabama's increase in welfare spending was the adoption—effective on the very day the program began—of federal funds for vendor payments to nursing homes that provided care to the state's old-age "pensioners." Vendor payments, in the terminology of welfare administration, are payments made directly to the vendor of services (i.e., the nursing home), rather than payments to clients for the purpose of meeting the costs of specified services. Prior to 1960, Alabama provided nursing-home care to recipients of its old-age assistance program (called "old-age pensions"), partly with federal funds given the state under an arrangement that demanded more state matching funds than were to be required under the 1960 amendments. Immediately, when the 1960 plan became available, the Alabama Department of Pensions and Security switched to the more lucrative matching formula. With the state appropriation that was freed by this transfer, the Department provided certain hospital services for its old-age pensioners. In effect, the state showed an increase in per capita welfare spending —a measure that includes federal funds received—which was greater than the increase in the spending of state funds for welfare.

While this account of a rapidly adopted federal program accounts for most of Alabama's abnormal 1961–1963 increase in welfare spending, it does not mention several factors of Alabama welfare policy which help to explain the state's ability to take such effective advantage of the new federal program. Compared to other components of its welfare program, Alabama's activities in old-age assistance score favorably in comparison to the efforts of other states. The state's orientation toward its pensioners, long a component of its political system, seems to have helped to prepare the Department of Pensions and Security to take immediate advantage of a new federal offering for the aged.

Like its neighboring states in the South, Alabama does not enjoy a reputation as a generous provider of welfare assistance. The state's economy is poor; and its population seems to take a conservative view toward the support of people who do not provide for their own needs. These factors of sparse resources and low service motivations seem to account for the low level of benefit payments given under the major public assistance programs of Old Age Assistance, Aid to Families of Dependent Children, Aid to the Blind, and Aid to the Permanently and Totally Disabled. Although Alabama payments under each of these programs are considerably lower than the national averages, the recipients of Old Age Assistance do relatively well. The figures below show that payments to pensioners—as the OAA recipients are labeled in Alabama—rank closest to the national average.

Alabama Average Benefits,
as Percentages of National Averages, 1965[2]

OAA: 85%       AFDC: 33%       AB: 74%       APTD: 54%

There are numerous other signs that Alabama treats its aged poor relatively well. The name of the program—Old Age Pensions—is designed to remove some of the welfare onus from the recipients. In order to provide fiinancial security to the old-age pensioners, the Alabama legislature has earmarked portions of six state taxes to the pension fund. The Old Age Pension program received $16.2 million (77 per cent of its total revenues) from earmarked sources during 1962 and 1963. The sources were liquor store profits and taxes on retail sales, on whiskey, on beer, on cigarettes, and on franchises. No other public assistance program in the state received more than $160,000 from earmarked sources.[3] Alabama politicians have respected the OAP program. Candidates for the governor's office generally advocate increases in benefits, and the eligibility requirements are liberal. Although a conservative Governor Persons successfully sponsored a law in the early 1950's which required that families of OAP recipients be responsible for some of their support, Jim Folsom made this an issue in his next gubernatorial campaign and repealed the law during the 1955 session of the legislature. Alabama's interest in assistance for the aged is particularly noticeable when the OAP program is compared to the AFDC program. The figures above show that old-age pensioners' *benefits* are more than twice as high—relative to national averages—as the benefits for dependent children. The following data, showing OAP recipient rates over three times as high as AFDC rates, suggest that eligibility requirements are far more liberal for OAP.

Alabama Average Recipient Rates,
as Percentages of National Averages, 1965[4]

OAP: 337%       AFDC: 96%       AB: 113%       APTD: 155%

Welfare officials in Alabama report that when the legislature is in session, they must be alert to guard the AFDC program against further

[2]Average benefits are recorded as average monthly payments, per recipient. The source of this data is the publication of the U.S. Department of Health, Education, and Welfare, *Social Welfare: Annual Statistical Supplement, 1965.*

[3]State of Alabama, Department of Pensions and Securities, *Annual Report, 1962–63.*

[4]The figures are recorded as OAA: number of recipients relative to the population over 65 years of age. For all other programs, the figures represent the number of recipients relative to the size of the total population. The source is U.S. Department of Health, Education, and Welfare, *Social Welfare: Annual Statistical Supplement, 1965.*

attacks by the lawmakers. An often-introduced provision would require the Department to suspend payments to a mother who gives birth to her second illegitimate child. Part of the problem faced by the AFDC program is racial in nature; Alabama politicians seem to have identified AFDC as a "Negro program." During the administration of Governor Patterson, welfare administrators felt it necessary to advertise among the legislators that 40 per cent of the AFDC recipients were white.

In contrast to other Alabama welfare programs, OAP seems to benefit from the respect given by the state to its unfortunate elderly. This class of the Alabama population receives the benefits of a program that is consciously mislabeled as a "pension program"; the rates and eligibility requirements are considerably more liberal than those applied to other welfare programs; and the state responded immediately to a new federal grant in behalf of the elderly.

When it came to adopting other federal offerings during the 1961–1963 period, the political and/or economic characteristics of Alabama seemed to deter major action. The state did not adopt a program to aid the dependent children of unemployed parents; and its program to provide medical assistance to persons not receiving old-age assistance has not gone beyond an insignificant number of beneficiaries. Although the medical program for the elderly might further Alabama's efforts to serve the needy aged, the expense of this program—if implemented on a large scale—would necessitate a much larger increase in state spending than the other recent innovations have required.

Rhode Island's experience during the 1963–1965 period illustrates another case where a state welfare department increased its expenditures in response to a federal program. However, between 1961 and 1963, Rhode Island also illustrates a set of conditions that led to a *delay* of three years in certain innovations beyond the time when they became available. Whereas Alabama's old-age program was operated in a way to make it profitable for the state to adopt generous 1960 amendments as soon as they became available, Rhode Island's program did not lend itself to a similar adoption. The Department of Social Welfare did not have such an established group of clients receiving nursing-home care that it could switch from one administrative category to another for the purpose of obtaining a more favorable ratio of federal-state expenditures. In 1961, Rhode Island officials considered adoption of a new program to provide medical care for aged persons who were not already on the welfare rolls (Medical Aid for the Aged). But the welfare department had previously committed itself to programs (involving less funds) to provide aid to the dependent children of unemployed workers and to reduce the case loads of its social workers. Welfare administrators felt that their capacity for innovation was completely absorbed by these programs, and they perceived that the Governor wanted to hold the line on major new expenditures. The Rhode Island Department of Social Welfare urged a deliberative course of action to the Governor and acceded to requests from legislators to study the experience of neighboring states before embarking on the new venture. By 1964, the welfare department felt itself capable of administering a new activity, and Governor John Chaffee lent his support to the required legislation. As a result, the state adopted an extensive program under Medical Care for the Aged which increased its expenditures per capita for public assistance from $24.29 to $26.94 in one year's time.[5] Between 1963 and 1965, Rhode Island's total welfare expenditures per capita increased from 117 to 143 per cent of the national average.

Along with Alabama and Rhode Island, a number of states showed upward deviations in their welfare spending during the 1961–1965 period which followed upon their adoption of new federal programs. In a number of cases, state welfare departments seem to have taken advantage of the innovative stimulus presented to certain programs by the new grants in order to revise other components of their programs. Maryland, for example, made major increases in average grants for each of the public assistance categories; and California liberalized the definition of "disability" in the program for Aid to the Permanently and Totally Disabled.

## SUMMARY

This chapter adds a different type of inquiry to the statistical analyses of state expenditures that is found in Chapters III–VII. By examining certain instances where the available statistical generalizations have performed poorly in estimating the expenditures of individual states, it has identified certain conditions that seem able to interrupt the normal association between past and current spending.

The cases reported here suggest that no single factor may lead a state to change its spending at a rate markedly above or below the national average. In the Kentucky upsurge of 1957–1962, the pro-spending Governor profited from a bonus bill that legislators passed. With the new revenue produced by the bonus-related sales tax, Governor Combs was able to spend at a level in 1962 that was almost 50 per cent higher than that predicted on the basis of 1957 spending. The Massachusetts 1957–1962 lag in spending illustrates a combination of conditions that hindered

---

[5]This specific increase in spending, attributed to the new MAA program, is described in a letter to the author from the Commissioner of Welfare, Augustine B. Riccio, February 14, 1967.

a state from moving ahead at the pace followed by the nation as a whole. Long-developing economic stagnation, an inclination toward private education, dependence upon an outmoded tax structure, and the intransigence of several governors and legislatures who blocked acceptance of new tax proposals worked together in holding down Massachusetts' spending. As part of the executive-legislative conflict it is reported that there was consistent underestimating of projected tax revenues. This tactic further substantiated the administration's claims that the state needed new revenue sources and may have held down the expenditure requests that agency heads were willing to assert.

While the contrasting experiences of Massachusetts and Kentucky during the 1957–1962 period does suggest that the availability of new revenues is at the heart of dramatic departures from nationwide rates of expenditure change, this conclusion would be hasty. Recalling the discussion surrounding Table III–8, it is apparent that the acquisition of a new tax base (or a major increase in tax rates) does not accompany dramatic spending increases in a consistent fashion. Moreover, the discussions of 1961–1965 welfare spending by Alabama and Rhode Island indicate that new revenues from the federal government do not by themselves stimulate uniform responses from the states.

The reports about Alabama and Rhode Island welfare departments suggest three factors that might intervene between the availability of a new federal program and an increase in state spending. These factors are: (1) the particular features of the federal legislation and the benefits they promise for the state program as it is currently administered; (2) the existing commitments of the state officials and the availability of organizational "slack" necessary to embark on a new venture; and (3) the attitudes of state officials toward the service to be rendered by the new federal funds. The Alabama case shows a state program already providing a large amount of the new federal program under a different financial scheme. By switching some administrative procedures, the Alabama Department of Pensions and Security could begin receiving a higher ratio of federal to state money and then use its released funds for complementary services. Behind this facile administrative maneuver was a long-standing bias in favor of welfare programs for the aged. Alabama's responses have not been as immediate to new federal programs for the families of dependent children; and the state's responses have not been as immediate to new programs for the aged that would require a substantial enlargement of its *own* expenditures. In Rhode Island, the Department of Social Welfare was not prepared for a major new program for the aged when the new federal funds became available. Its top administrators committed resources to other, less costly innovations, and the

Governor wanted to avoid new increases in state spending. Unlike Alabama, Rhode Island did not have an established program where a simple shift in administrative procedures would increase the ratio of federal to state money. Rhode Island chose to be deliberative about the new medical programs for the aged, and its welfare expenditures did not show a dramatic rise until it adopted the new Medical Care program during the 1963–1965 period. Thus, the motivations of officials and their administrative exigencies seem to rival new revenue sources as factors that can have critical influence on the spending decisions of state governments.

CHAPTER IX

# Systems Theory, Incrementalism, and State Government Expenditures

THIS BOOK has tried to unite two levels of analysis: (1) an introductory discussion of political theories that pertain to state government expenditures, and (2) a quantitative analysis of expenditures and related phenomena. As described in Chapter I, a *political system* consists of a set of relationships that produce expressions of desire and the selection among competing desires by authorities who determine public policies. Government expenditures, presumably, are the substance of authoritative decisions to spend public revenues. Expenditures appear central to the full range of authoritative decisions, insofar as they provide the wherewithal to purchase and maintain the services, regulations, and capital facilities that are authorized according to the orderly process of official decisions.[1] As viewed in the context of systems theory, expenditures seem likely to reflect the economic, social, and political forces that operate upon state governments. When measures of state and local government expenditures have been examined in "systems" models that have tested for the relative influence of economic and political phenomena, the economic influences have outweighed such political influences as voter turnout, the strength of major political parties, and the equity of apportionment in the state legislature.[2] Incrementalists, however, have viewed

[1]Robert C. Wood, *1400 Governments* (Garden City, N.Y.: Anchor Books, 1961); Philip H. Burch, Jr., *Highway Revenue and Expenditure Policy in the United States* (New Brunswick, N.J.: Rutgers University Press, 1962); Jesse Burkhead, *Public School Finance* (Syracuse, N.Y.: Syracuse University Press, 1964).

[2]Richard E. Dawson and James A. Robinson, "Interparty Competition, Economic Variables, and Welfare Policies in the American States," *Journal of Politics,* 25

government expenditures as an integral part of a political process. They are "incrementalists" because they share the view that the increment between previous expenditures and current requests is the major ingredient in the determination of current spending levels. Although previous expenditure is a political concept that reflects habits, past accommodations, and the conservative orientation of government budget procedures, incrementalists occasionally describe the past-present spending relationship as being almost apolitical in nature: decision-makers feeding largely off their own previous decisions in relative isolation from other political or economic phenomena.[3]

One of the purposes served by Chapters III to VIII of this book has been the evaluation of state government expenditures with respect to systems theory and incrementalism. The focus has been the question: Why do some state governments spend more money than others? Thus, the analysis has faced, in sequence, a series of phenomena that stand as potential influences on state spending: the level of previous expenditures; other governmental and political characteristics of the state; socio-economic characteristics; historical experiences of depression, war, and post-war reconversion; regional affiliation of states; demands for public services; and peculiarities of state economics, politics, and administration that help to explain spending changes that deviate from general patterns.

The essential findings of Chapters III to VIII with respect to current expenditures per capita may be summarized as follows:

(1) The single factor that shows the closest relationship to state government expenditures in a current year is the level of expenditures during the recent past.

(2) Aside from the level of previous expenditures, the following characteristics of state governments generally show *positive* relationships with current spending:

(a) a high proportion of state revenues received as federal aid;

(b) a high proportion of citizens' income paid into state taxes;

---

(May 1963): 265–89; Richard I. Hofferbert, "The Relation between Public Policy and Some Structural and Environmental Variables in the American States," *American Political Science Review*, 60 (March 1966): 73–82; and Thomas R. Dye, *Politics, Economics, and the Public: Policy Outcomes in the American States* (Chicago: Rand McNally & Co., 1966).

[3]Charles Lindblom, "Decision-Making in Taxation and Expenditure," in National Bureau of Economic Research, *Public Finances: Needs, Sources, and Utilization* (Princeton, N.J.: Princeton University Press, 1961); Thomas J. Anton, *The Politics of State Expenditure in Illinois* (Urbana: University of Illinois Press, 1966); Aaron Wildavsky, *The Politics of the Budgetary Process* (Boston: Little, Brown & Co., 1964); and John P. Crecine, "A Computer Simulation Model of Municipal Resource Allocation" (paper read at a meeting of the Midwest Conference of Political Science, April 1966).

      (c) a large state bureaucracy, relative to population;

      (d) a high share of state-local financial responsibilities assumed by the state government.

(3) The following characteristics of states show *negative* relationships with current spending:

      (a) population;

      (b) urbanization;

      (c) industrialization.

(4) When the current spending in American states is examined on a regional basis, the following generalizations appear:

      (a) states in northern and eastern regions tend to spend below the national average for the services of education, highways, and natural resources, but above the national average for health and hospitals and public safety;

      (b) states in western regions tend to spend above the national average for most fields of public service;

      (c) states in southern regions spend at levels that do not deviate appreciably from the national average.

(5) Measures pertaining to the relationships between citizens and governments (voter turnout, party strength, interparty competition, and the nature of state legislatures) show only weak relationships with current spending.

(6) Contrary to the assumptions of prominent economists and political scientists, there is no consistent relationship between levels of public services and the combined expenditures of state and local governments.

The findings about correlates of *changes in spending,* as opposed to current spending, warn that answers from a static analysis of expenditures do not transfer readily to an analysis of change. This warning has two implications:

(1) Characteristics associated with current levels of spending in a positive (or negative) fashion may not provoke increases (or decreases) with respect to the existing level of expenditures.

(2) The relationships between current levels of spending and the independent variables reported for 1962 may not appear in comparable analyses of earlier or later years.[4]

The dynamic character of state government expenditures is apparent throughout this book. While previous expenditures exert a powerful influence over current budget decisions, their weight has not precluded

[4]See Richard I. Hofferbert, "Stability and Change in Some Social Correlates of Political Participation and Policy Outputs in the States" (paper read at the annual meeting of the Southwestern Social Science Association, Dallas, 1967).

great increases in state spending throughout this century. The essential findings of this book with respect to changes in expenditures are as follows:

(1) Changes in expenditures are seldom so dramatic as to upset prevailing differences between the spending of various states.

(2) The fluctuating nature of expenditure change permits state governments to alternate between periods of increase and periods of stability and thereby maintain relative differences among themselves.

(3) During the 1962–1965 period, characteristics associated with high scores in expenditure growth include high scores on measures of federal aid, tax effort, and the state share of state-local financial obligations and low scores on measures of population, urbanization, and industrialization.

(4) Throughout the twentieth century there has been a tendency for the gap between high- and low-spending states to narrow. This narrowing proceeded most rapidly during the depression years of 1929–1939. Between 1962 and 1965, the gap between high- and low-spending states increased; but this departure from the prevailing pattern is limited to the field of highway expenditures, where major federal grants may have been a more powerful stimulant for some states than others.

(5) In comparison with spending for common functions by the federal and local governments, state spending for these functions increased between 1902 and the depression, remained stable during the depression, decreased during World War II and the Korean Conflict, and increased again in postwar years.

(6) Regional norms seem to play a role in state spending by providing targets for budget-makers. Throughout the century, the spending patterns of states in specific regions have been more uniform than the spending of states in the nation as a whole.

(7) Although most regions have retained stable spending levels (relative to national averages) throughout most of the century, states in the Southwest showed significant increases in spending following World War I; states of the Southeast increased their spending following World War II; and states in the Northeast have exhibited a decline in their spending since World War II.

(8) Insofar as the present collection of independent variables leaves unexplained much of the interstate variation in measures of expenditure change, there is considerable opportunity for the motivations and political resources of individuals or organizations, as well as peculiarities of state economics and social characteristics, to effect changes in spending.

The findings of this book may have both *petit* and *gran* relevance for systems theory. From a narrow viewpoint, the findings document the relationships between spending by American states and a series of phenomena that have relevance for systems theory: characteristics of government, politics, and economics; historical experiences; regional culture; the demands for public services; and the motivations and strengths of individuals and groups. From a wider viewpoint, the findings may help explain the general function assigned to expenditures within political systems and/or the contributions that political systems allegedly make to economic and social systems.

This book by itself can do little more than pose the question for the larger view. The data and analyses of Chapters III to VIII pertain only to the American states. For a number of reasons that are mentioned in Chapter II, it is not feasible without further research to expand the findings to financial decision-making outside of this context. In other political units that have different service responsibilities or exist in different economic, political, or social milieus than the American states, budget-makers may respond integrally to the stimuli of current economics or the characteristics pertaining to citizen-government relationships. However, to the extent that expenditure decisions in the American states and elsewhere are isolated from political or economic phenomena by a fixation on their own past appropriations, the conception of a responsive, integrated political system is misleading.

This book makes no effort to pose a debate between systems theory and incrementalism. These theories represent separate, but not mutually exclusive, frames of reference which have helped to guide the analysis. The publications about budget-making, which describe the incremental techniques pursued by decision-makers, help to explain the statistical relationships between current expenditures and those of the recent past which outweigh the relationships between current expenditures and numerous measures of economic, social, governmental, and political characteristics that are designed to reflect the concepts that are typically considered in systems approaches. Insofar as humans are bound by habit and routine, the present mirrors the past in many activities of individuals and governments. However, the budgetary process, in particular, includes a set of well-developed procedures that formalize and reinforce the influence of the past over the present. Thomas J. Anton describes the activities of state budget officers in Illinois as fixing their inquiries upon last year's expenditures and upon the increment of change included in the current request.[5] Generally speaking, budgeteers in the agencies, administrative review bodies, and the legislature pass over programmatic considerations for criteria that focus upon the number of dollars to be spent.

[5]See Anton, *Politics of State Expenditure.*

Except for a commitment to "economizing" (i.e., budget-cutting), financial decision-makers tend to ignore ideology. Neither the nature of the economy nor the programs of victorious candidates are likely to have a general influence over the many decisions that produce a state's budget. Aaron Wildavsky and Charles Lindblom provide explanations for the narrow budget perspective.[6] Budgeteers lack the time, training, and/or inclination to evaluate all the program considerations latent in any agency's proposal. Lacking the resources to make independent investigations, they accept the previous budget as an agency's "legitimate" appropriations and concentrate upon the implications arising from the difference between last year's allocations and that (generally an increase) proposed. Lindblom and Wildavsky commend incrementalism as a decisional process that narrows the focus of program consideration to manageable proportions. As Anton describes incrementalism in Illinois budgeting, the focus is even more narrowly upon differences in dollar sums with little opportunity for agencies to admit their claims for program expansion into the budget process itself. The difference between the Wildavsky and Anton descriptions of incrementalism may reflect the difference between the resources devoted to executive and legislative budget scrutiny at the federal and state levels. The Federal Bureau of the Budget and the Congressional Appropriations Committees (the subjects of Wildavsky's analysis) are better supplied with staff skills and opportunities for continuous involvement in budgeting than is the case for comparable bodies in most state governments. As a result, federal officials are more likely than state officials to go beyond a consideration of dollars to a consideration of the activities to be purchased with the dollars.

The most severe analytical limitation shown by incrementalism lies in its inability to clarify changes in the levels of spending. Increasing levels of expenditure, no less than stability of interstate differentials in spending, are a component of state governments' recent history. Much of the change examined in this book seems to be provoked by generalized phenomena that affect most states at the same time: depression, war, postwar reconversion, inflation, and the enlargement of real economic resources. The independent variables of Chapters III and IV are less successful in accounting for changes in expenditures than in accounting for the level of current spending. The stimulants of specific changes in spending include both the general phenomena noted above and particularistic or transient occurrences; neither lend themselves to quantification as independent variables. The generalized phenomena do not vary

[6]See Lindblom, "Decision-Making," and Wildavsky, *Politics of the Budgetary Process.*

markedly in their impact from one state to another; and the particularistic factors do not adapt to comparable measurement from one state to the next.

Systems theory has helped in the search for the stimulants of change by suggesting the relevance of *resources, rules, needs, demands,* and *motivations.* The resources that appear important to changes in spending are the federal grants-in-aid and the willingness of citizens to continue paying a certain percentage of their income into state taxes. Salient rules include those that set the limits of states' (as opposed to localities') responsibilities for the provision of public services, as well as the provisions included in federal grant programs that require states to support a certain proportion of a project's costs with their own resources. The needs that may help to generate increases in state spending are reflected in the low scores on measures of "economic development" which accompany measures of recent increases in spending. The data of Chapter IV show that predominantly rural, non-industrial, low-population states tended to show the greatest spending increases during the 1962–1965 period. Moreover, the discussion in Chapter V indicates that the economic need of local authorities was a stimulus of the enlarged state role during the depression. While citizens' demands for public services do not seem to have a positive influence on government spending (as described in Chapter VII), these demands may occasionally receive critical support from elected officials. Although no quantitative measure of motivation appears in this book, the discussion of Kentucky's great spending surge between 1957 and 1962 suggests that a highly placed, highly motivated official who perceives the needs for increased services and expenditures can be a potent force in state budgeting, despite the dampening effect of incremental budgeting.

Any understanding of the state expenditure process must reckon with two basic ingredients: the conservative bias of incrementalism; and the numerous pressures that work to increase spending. By illustrating that spending has increased greatly during this century and that interstate spending differentials have persisted over several decades, this book has described a process that is open and flexible and, at the same time, has great respect for the past.

## INFLUENCES UPON DECISIONS: ECONOMICS, POLITICS, AND THE PAST

Both the assumptions of incrementalism and the substantive findings of this book argue against the claims of certain writers that economics, above all, exercises dominant influence over the outputs of state (and local) governments.[7] The same limitations of time and intelligence that affect budgeteers are likely to influence officials who make policy decisions about tax rates and the nature of services provided in the fields of education, welfare, health, public safety, *et al*. With few exceptions, it seems unlikely that administrators, executives, or legislators examine the entirety of agency programs. Established activities have legitimacy and probably receive no more than a cursory acknowledgment while reviewers examine unmet needs and proposed innovations. Across the full range of government programs, the factors likely to correspond most with current levels of activity are previous levels of activity.[8]

Writers who emphasize the economic correlates of public programs do not deny the influence of previous levels of activity. Rather, they ignore the influence of past decisions while seeking the constellation of factors that show strong relationships with current operations. When they claim that economics, more than politics, affects government outputs, they look past an obvious happening in the governmental process: the practice of public officials to accept established expenditures, taxes, or services and make decisions only about proposed modifications.

The finding that previous decisions are the most salient considerations in making present decisions has obvious implications for reform proposals. Two possible types of reform are at issue: (1) the use of budget mechanisms to achieve reforms in economic, political, or social systems; and (2) the reform of budget mechanisms themselves.

The operational "distance" between the budgetary system and characteristics of other systems considered in this book does not hold much promise for the use of budgeting as a vehicle for change in the United States. While spending decisions occasionally have telling influence upon external phenomena, the nature of state budgeting criteria makes success unlikely for any particular effort. The weak relationship between changes in spending and changes in services suggests that the expected linkages between an expenditure change and a service change may fail to occur; and a concerted effort to produce a marked deviation from established spending seems unlikely to succeed. Among the states (and perhaps elsewhere in the world), the budget process serves a conservative function amidst political and economic systems. The reformer, with a vision of change, must be an optimist as he approaches a public budget-maker. As described by Wildavsky and Anton, the budget system is populated not by officials with compelling program sympathies, but by officials who

[7]See the works cited above in note 2.
[8]The author has found this to be true in tests with several of the educational and welfare service indicators used in Chapter VII.

elevate their own past decisions to the status of principal decision criteria.

What are the prospects of change in the budget mechanisms themselves? How good are the chances that a reformer can oust incrementalism from public budgeting? Can the rational-comprehensive style, with its consideration of every budget item and all cogent alternatives, become operational?

The results of this and other examinations of government spending in the United States indicate that budget mechanisms may satisfy at least as many actors as they antagonize.[9] Budgetary processes that respect the past may have a peculiar appeal in the midst of an ongoing pluralistic struggle for change. As a conservative bulwark, the budget may encourage legislators, administrators, and private groups to tolerate competition for change because no *radical* change is likely to survive the funding process. If the superficial mechanics of budgeting are altered, it is possible that budget-makers (with the encouragement of outsiders) will operate a new machine essentially as they operate now—with the base of past spending and incrementalism.[10]

No assessment of possible changes in budgeting procedure can fail to reckon with its complex techniques. There is a lead-time of many months within the budgeting process. At the federal level, 27 months elapse between the beginning of budget-making and the end of the budget (fiscal) year. In states with biennial appropriations, the gap between the agencies' first decisions about their requests and the final expenditures is considerably longer. Within this span of time, actors operate formally under authority derived from several statutes or executive orders and informally under procedures devised by legislators and administrators. They fill the time with highly technical paperwork and a number of deadlines. Without detailed procedural knowledge, a reformer would not know how and where to apply his modifications.[11] It may be an exaggeration to cite the esoteric nature of budgeting as the feature that isolates it from other economic, political, and social systems. Budgeting is not a world to itself, and budgeteers are not priest-like in their control of mysterious formulas and incantations. However, neither laymen nor many officials seem anxious to learn the internal processes of budgeting. Thus, the mystery of budgeting may be one factor that makes the outputs of current spending so important as inputs for subsequent decisions.

[9]See Anton's discussion of the Illinois budget system's "victory" over a governor who, early in his administration, had sought major financial changes: *Politics of State Expenditure*, p. 140.

[10]Aaron Wildavsky, "Political Implications of Budgetary Reform," *Public Administration Review*, 21 (Autumn 1961): 183–90.

[11]Anton, *Politics of State Expenditure*, pp. 236–40.

APPENDIX

# A Listing of Variables with Their Sources

IN THIS APPENDIX, the variables are listed in the approximate order of their appearance in the tables of Chapters III–VII. Unless it is otherwise noted, all of the publications listed below come from the U.S. Government Printing Office in Washington, D.C. Many of the variables used in this book are not found in the following sources in the same form in which they are analyzed. To fit the purposes of various inquiries, it has been necessary to combine several "raw" measures, to correct them for population size or other "control" variables, or to invert them (i.e., transpose high and low scores without altering interstate variations) in order to make them consistent with other variables used in a particular inquiry. This Appendix identifies the source of each variable. When checking the raw data for individual states against the findings, the reader must be careful to correct the raw data to correspond with the variables used in this book.

| Variable | Source |
|---|---|
| (1) General expenditures per capita, in total and by major field, 1903–1965 | The data pertaining to 1903 and 1933 come from the Census Bureau publication *Wealth, Debt and Taxation, 1913;* the data pertaining to 1918–1939 come from each year's Census Bureau publication, *Financial Statistics of States.* Beginning with 1942 and continuing to 1965, the data come from the Census Bureau's *Compendium of State Government Finances.* |

SOCIO-ECONOMIC MEASURES

| | |
|---|---|
| (2) Total personal income, 1962 | U.S. Bureau of the Census, *Statistical Abstract of the United States, 1964.* |
| (3) Personal income per capita, 1962 | *Ibid.* |
| (4) Percentage of population in urban areas, 1960 | *Ibid.* |
| (5) Population, 1962 | *Ibid.* |
| (6) Percentage growth in population, 1957–1962 | *Ibid.*, and *Statistical Abstract, 1957.* |
| (7) Percentage of labor force employed in manufacturing, 1958–1959 | U.S. Bureau of the Census, *City-County Data Book, 1962.* |
| (8) Value added by manufacture per capita, 1958 | *Ibid.* |
| (9) Percentage of adults (25 years of age and over) with at least four years of college, 1960 | *Statistical Abstract, 1964.* |
| (10) Percentage of families with annual incomes of less than $2,000, 1960 | *Ibid.* |
| (11) Population per square mile, 1962 | *Ibid.* |
| (12) Area in square miles | *Ibid.* |
| (13) Percentage of labor force *not* employed in farming, fishing, and forestry, 1960 | *Ibid.* |
| (14) Percentage of population that is non-white, 1960 | *Ibid.* |
| (15) Percentage of population foreign-born, or native-born of foreign or mixed parentage, 1960 | *Ibid.* |

POLITICAL MEASURES

| | |
|---|---|
| (16) Percentage of voting-age population voting in 1962 | *Ibid.* |

election for U.S. Representative

(17) Percentage of voting-age population voting in the 1962 (or 1960) gubernatorial election — *Ibid.*

(18) Percentage of seats in lower house of state legislature occupied by majority party, 1962 — *Ibid.*

(19) Percentage of seats in upper house of state legislature occupied by majority party, 1962 — *Ibid.*

(20) Percentage of votes received by majority party in 1962 election for U.S. Representative — *Ibid.*

(21) Percentage of votes received by winner in 1962 (or 1960) gubernatorial election — *Ibid.*

(22) Number of years in 1952–1962 period that majority party held governor's office — *Ibid.*

(23) Average salary of state legislators, 1962–1963 — Council of State Governments, *The Book of the States, 1964–65* (Chicago, 1964).

(24) Number of bills introduced in a session of the state legislature, 1962–1963 — *Ibid.*

(25) Number of bills passed in a session of the state legislature, 1962–1963 — *Ibid.*

(26) Number of days in a session of the state legislature, 1962–1963 — *Ibid.*

(27) Expenditures for support of the state legislature in a biennium, exclusive of legislators' compensation, 1962–1963

*Ibid.*

(28) Schubert-Press (corrected) index of malapportionment

*American Political Science Review,* 58 (1964): 969.

(29) Dauer-Kelsay index of malapportionment

Paul T. David and Ralph Eisenberg, *Devaluation of the Urban and Suburban Vote* (Charlottesville: Bureau of Public Administration, University of Virginia, 1961), p. 5.

(30) David-Eisenberg index of malapportionment

*Ibid.,* p. 15.

(31) Number of years during 1954–1962 period majority party held control of the lower house of the state legislature

*Statistical Abstract, 1964.*

(32) Number of years during 1954–1962 period majority party held control of the upper house of the state legislature

*Ibid.*

(33) Number of state legislators, 1962–1963

*Ibid.*

GOVERNMENTAL MEASURES

(34) Percentage of state revenue received through federal aid, 1962

*Compendium of State Government Finances, 1962.*

(35) Percentage of residents' personal income paid in state taxes, 1962

*Ibid.*

(36) State personal-income-tax receipts per capita, 1962

*Ibid.*

(37) State general-sales-tax receipts per capita, 1962

*Ibid.*

(38) State excise-tax receipts per capita, 1962     *Ibid.*

(39) Personal income tax as a percentage of total taxes, 1962     *Ibid.*

(40) General sales tax as a percentage of total taxes, 1962     *Ibid.*

(41) Excise tax as a percentage of total taxes, 1962     *Ibid.*

(42) State percentage of state and local government expenditures, 1962     *Statistical Abstract, 1964.*

(43) Percentage of state and local government revenues allocated to state, 1962     U.S. Bureau of the Census, *Census of Governments, 1962,* and *Compendium of State Government Finances.*

(44) Percentage of state and local government revenues derived from non-local sources, 1962     *Ibid.*

(45) Local government expenditures per capita, 1962     *Ibid.*

(46) Average salary of state government employees, 1962     *Statistical Abstract, 1964.*

(47) Number of state government employees per 10,-000 population, 1962     *Ibid.*

## EDUCATIONAL MEASURES

(48) Pupils per classroom teacher, 1961     National Education Association, *Rankings of the States, 1963* (Washington, 1963).

(49) Percentage of elementary-school teachers with at least a bachelor's degree, 1961     *Ibid.*

(50) Percentage of secondary-school teachers with at least a master's degree, 1961

*Ibid.*

(51) Total enrollment in federally aided vocational education per 10,000 population, 1961, 1957

*Statistical Abstract, 1964* and *1958.*

(52) Percentage of school enrollment participating in the federal school lunch program, 1963, 1957

*Ibid.*

(53) Number of persons in process of vocational rehabilitation per 10,000 population, 1961, 1957

*Ibid.*

(54) Number of persons completing vocational rehabilitation per 10,000 population, 1961, 1957

*Ibid.*

(55) Average percentage of students in daily attendance at elementary and secondary schools, 1962

U.S. Office of Education, *Digest of Educational Statistics, 1964.*

(56) Length of school term, 1960

*Statistical Abstract, 1964.*

(57) Population per school district, 1961–1962

*Digest of Educational Statistics, 1964.*

(58) Percentage of ninth-graders who graduated from high school three years later, 1957–1958, 1960–1961.

*Rankings of the States, 1963* and *1965.*

(59) Percentage of selective-service inductees passing mental exam, 1961, 1963.

*Ibid.*

(60) Earned master's degrees per 10,000 population conferred by all institu-

*Digest of Educational Statistics, 1964,* and *Statistical Abstract, 1960.*

tions of higher education,
1962–1963, 1958

(61) Earned doctorates per 10,000 population conferred by all institutions of higher education, 1962–1963, 1958

*Ibid.*

(62) Enrollment in institutions of higher education per 10,000 population, 1963, 1957

*Digest of Educational Statistics, 1964,* and *Statistical Abstract, 1960.*

(63) Enrollment of natives in their own states' institutions of higher education per 10,000 population, 1963

*Digest of Educational Statistics, 1964.*

## Highway Measures

(64) Mileage per capita of state-administered roads, 1962, 1958

*The Book of the States, 1964–65* and *1960–61.*

(65) Mileage per rural resident of state-administered rural roads, 1962, 1957

*Statistical Abstract, 1964* and *1959.*

(66) Mileage per urban resident of municipal roads, 1962, 1957

*Ibid.*

(67) Percentage of farms on paved roads, 1959

U.S. Bureau of the Census, *Census of Agriculture, 1959.*

(68) Percentage of four- or six-lane miles in federally aided mileage completed during 1963, 1957

U.S. Bureau of Public Roads, *Annual Report, 1963,* and *Annual Highway Statistics, 1957.*

(69) Mileage per capita of interstate highways open to traffic, 1962

*Statistical Abstract, 1964.*

(70) Percentage of designated interstate mileage completed by 1962

*Ibid.*

(71) Percentage of designated interstate mileage completed or in progress during 1962

Bureau of Public Roads, *Annual Report, 1963.*

(72) State residents per motor vehicle death, 1962, 1956

*Statistical Abstract, 1964* and *1958.*

## PUBLIC WELFARE MEASURES

(73) Number of people over 65 years old, 1960, 1956

*Ibid.*

(74) Incidence of recipients of Old Age Assistance in relation to people over 65 years old with annual incomes of less than $2,000, 1963, 1957

*Ibid.*

(75) Incidence of recipients of Medical Assistance for the Aged in relation to people over 65 years old with annual incomes of less than $2,000, 1963, 1957

*Ibid.*

(76) Incidence of recipients of Aid to Families with Dependent Children in relation to people with annual incomes of less than $2,-000, 1963, 1957

*Ibid.*

(77) Incidence of recipients of Aid to the Blind in relation to people with annual incomes of less than $2,-000, 1963, 1957

*Ibid.*

(78) Incidence of recipients of Aid to the Permanently and Totally Disabled in relation to people with annual incomes of less than $2,000, 1963, 1957

*Ibid.*

(79) Average payment per recipient of OAA, 1963, 1957

*Statistical Abstract, 1964; The Book of the States, 1958–59.*

(80) Average payment per recipient of AFDC, 1963, 1957

*Ibid.*

(81) Average payment per recipient of AB, 1963, 1957

*Ibid.*

(82) Average payment per recipient of APTD, 1963, 1957

*Ibid.*

(83) Number of children, per 10,000 child population, receiving child welfare benefits, 1963

*Statistical Abstract, 1964.*

## HEALTH AND HOSPITAL MEASURES

(84) Number of hospital beds per 10,000 population, 1962

*Ibid.*

(85) Number of hospital bassinets per 10,000 population, 1962, 1957

*Ibid.* and *Statistical Abstract, 1959.*

(86) Number of patients, per 10,000 population, in mental hospitals, 1961, 1957

*Statistical Abstract, 1964* and *1960.*

(87) Net number of patients released alive from mental hospitals (live releases minus returning patients), 1961

*Statistical Abstract, 1964.*

(88) Number of patients, per 10,000 population, in institutions for mental defectives and epileptics, 1958

*Statistical Abstract, 1961.*

(89) Number of physicians per 100,000 population, 1962, 1957

*Statistical Abstract, 1964* and *1958.*

(90) Number of dentists per 100,000 population, 1962, 1957

*Ibid.*

(91) State residents per the number of children found to be disabled, 1963

U.S. Social Security Administration, *Social Security Bulletin, 1963.*

(92) Number of deaths of white infants under one year of age, per 1,000 live births, 1962, 1957

*Statistical Abstract, 1964* and *1959.*

(93) Number of deaths of non-white infants under one year of age, per 1,000 live births, 1962, 1957

*Ibid.*

## NATURAL RESOURCE MEASURES

(94) Number of cooperative extension agents per 10,-000 population, 1962, 1957

*The Book of the States, 1964–65* and *1958–59.*

(95) Number of agricultural experiment station researchers per 10,000 population, 1962, 1956

*Ibid.*

(96) Total farm acreage, 1959

*Statistical Abstract, 1964.*

(97) Percentage of farm acreage in soil conservation districts, 1963, 1957

*Ibid.* and *Statistical Abstract, 1958.*

(98) Percentage of total acreage mapped within soil conservation districts, 1961

U.S. Department of Agriculture, *Agriculture Statistics, 1962.*

(99) Percentage of cropland in Agricultural Conservation Program, 1960

*Ibid.*

(100) Acreage per capita of state parks, 1962, 1956

*Statistical Abstract, 1964* and *1958.*

(101) Acreage per visitor of state parks, 1962, 1956

*Ibid.*

(102) Visitors to state parks per 10,000 population, 1962, 1956

*The Book of the States, 1964–65* and *1958–59*.

(103) Number of fishing licenses sold per 10,000 population, 1962, 1957

*Statistical Abstract, 1964* and *1958*.

(104) Number of hunting licenses sold per 10,000 population, 1962, 1957

*Ibid.*

## PUBLIC SAFETY MEASURES

(105) Offenses, per 100,000 population, of murder and non-negligent manslaughter, 1962, 1957

F.B.I., *Uniform Crime Rates for the United States, 1963;* and *Statistical Abstract, 1959.*

(106) Offenses, per 100,000 population, of forcible rape, 1962, 1957

*Ibid.*

(107) Offenses, per 100,000 population, of robbery, 1962, 1957

*Ibid.*

(108) Offenses, per 100,000 population, of aggravated assault, 1962, 1957

*Ibid.*

(109) Offenses, per 100,000 population, of burglary or breaking and entering, 1962, 1957

*Ibid.*

(110) Offenses, per 100,000 population, of larceny ($50 and over), 1962, 1957

*Ibid.*

(111) Offenses, per 100,000 population, of auto theft, 1962, 1957

*Ibid.*

(112) Percentage conditional releases of total releases from correctional institutions, 1964, 1957

U.S. Bureau of Prisons, *National Prisoner Statistics, 1965* and *1957*.

(113) Percentage of conditional releases not returned to correctional institutions as violators, 1964, 1957

*Ibid.*

(114–21) State and local government expenditures, in total and by major field, 1962, 1957

*Census of Governments, 1962* and *1957;* and *Compendium of Government Finances, 1962* and *1957.*

# INDEX

PRINTED IN U.S.A.